BETTING ON TWO YEAR OLDS

The Inside Track

Nick Attenborough

© 2009 Nick Attenborough
Betting on Two Year Olds
The Inside Track

ISBN 978-0-9562136-0-0

Published by Inside Track
PO Box 65107
LONDON
SW1P 9PP
www.insidetrack.me

A CIP catalogue record of this book
can be obtained from the British Library.

Book designed by Michael Walsh at
THE BETTER BOOK COMPANY

A division of
RPM Print & Design
2-3 Spur Road
Chichester
West Sussex
PO19 8PR

Cover photograph: See In The Dark, Windsor, July 2006
by Anne Richardson

INDEX

ACKNOWLEDGEMENTS

I would like to thank all those in the racing industry who have contributed information to this book. Particular thanks are due to Brian and Kim Meehan, Johnny McKeever, Sam Bullard, Grace Muir, Jeremy Wray, Marbeth Blair, Jon Ryan, Owen Byrne, and Barbara Fitzgerald. I would also like to thank all the jockeys who responded to my request for a quote. I must also acknowledge *Raceform* and *The Racing Post*; I wouldn't bet without them. I would especially like to thank my sister Claire for her comments and her patience in typing several versions of this manuscript and my wife, Anne, for her drafting skills. All these contributions were invaluable.

INTRODUCTION

When I first started betting on horses as a teenager, some forty years ago, I became fascinated by the challenges of finding two year old winners.

In those early days there was, of course, the Form Book and Timeform for those who could afford them, but there was scant little else to guide the novice punter trying to sort juvenile winners from no-hopers.

Nowadays, form students face a world of difference. In addition to the historical racing form in the newspapers, we have easy access to a wealth of useful statistics: TV footage of every race, racing websites at our fingertips and a well-informed media that provide pages of in-depth analysis, copious comment and critique.

Furthermore, the UK betting market has been revolutionised in recent years with the advent of betting exchanges and, in particular, Betfair. Nowadays, ordinary punters have the choice of backing the selection they believe will win or laying runners that they believe cannot win, like conventional bookmakers.

The problem with backing or laying two year olds, despite the availability of advice from the media, is that, unlike other forms of racing, there aren't many hard facts to guide us. In many races, two year old runners are either lightly raced or they are having a first outing at the racecourse. The lack of information leads to the creation of false favourites – a nightmare for the punters.

Despite this, there are some strong clues that can make finding a winner much easier whilst also providing fantastic trading opportunities for those who like to lay horses on the exchanges. So, if you think that two year old racing is trickier form-wise than finding winners on virtual racing at Sprint Valley or Steeple-downs, then read on.

For starters, two year olds are, in the main, much more consistent than older flat horses. They may lack experience but they are also less likely to have picked up bad habits. It is worth remembering that horses in the wild live in herds and they use flight as their escape mechanism. Horse racing capitalises on this instinct. But once the lesson has been learnt that the racecourse is relatively safe, the reasons for running flat out can diminish. As racehorses get older some of them can get soured by racing – they can 'save a bit for themselves.' In other words, some start to understand that life doesn't end if they don't exert themselves fully.

Second, is the fact that there are far fewer two year olds than horses of other ages. In 2008, for example, just over 3,200 two year olds competed in some 1050 races during the turf season (the two year old races that take place between late March and early November). Although these numbers are pretty daunting and they are significantly higher than 30 years ago, the actual number of two year old races, compared to 1979, has only increased by about 20 per cent. By contrast, the data and media available to help us understand what's going on have increased vastly.

Third, and also on the positive side is the fact that most horses will progress consistently throughout their juvenile year, and most juveniles continue to grow in both size and strength during the season. They therefore improve as a result. As two year olds race almost entirely against their own age, there's not the added complication of trying to weigh up the relative merits of different generations.

Fourth, performance comparisons are a great deal easier throughout the juvenile season. The majority of two year old races are over sprint distances (over 60 per cent of races are over five or six furlongs) so it is a relatively straightforward matter to compare one with another. But two year olds can also get soured by hard races or by being over-raced: racing week-in, week-out will exhaust even the best horse.

There's now so much racing that it's almost impossible to keep tabs on all aspect of the turf. However, two year old racing is so more manageable than the rest. There are far fewer runners to focus on and relatively few races every day, so detailed form study is made significantly easier. This book aims to crystallise what I've learnt over the years from studying and analysing two year old form, combined with my anecdotal experience as a racehorse owner. I aim to help you use the probabilities and the evidence to increase the likelihood that your trading on two year olds is successful.

Over the past twenty five years, I've been very fortunate to have owned a number of successful two year olds with some of the UK's most talented flat trainers: Brian Meehan, David Elsworth, Mick Channon and

Peter Cundell. This has taught me an amazing amount about the trials and tribulations of owning two year olds. It's also provided me with winners almost every season including with good horses such as *Siena Gold*, winner of the Weatherbys Super Sprint at Newbury; *Wave Aside*, unlucky not to have won the Redcar Two Year Old Trophy and *Amaretto Bay*, winner of the National Stakes at Sandown. I've also had my fair share of slower animals which have, in their own way, provided insights into backing and laying two year olds.

In this book, I have tried to condense that learning into key facts which I believe are a major influence on a two year old's chance of winning or losing.

CHAPTER I

The Two Year Old Season

THE TWO YEAR OLD SEASON

The racing season for two year olds is a markedly different experience than the racing season for older horses. It is important to understand this, and appreciate the subtle step changes that occur throughout the turf racing year. Why? Because they impact significantly on race outcomes and upon the success of your predictions. In this chapter, I list the most important races in the calendar and the essential things you should know.

March

The season for juveniles invariably kicks off with the Brocklesby Stakes, a five furlong cavalry charge for mostly unraced two year olds over Doncaster's straight course. The race tends to attract quite a few above-average, early season two year olds since the prize money is good for the time of year. Trainers tend to run their stronger and better early types here. By contrast, the remaining March two year old races tend only to attract the more moderate horses that have come to hand early. It therefore pays to respect any Brocklesby runners that appear in the later races. The probability is that they are the better horses.

April

In April, two year old racing steps up a gear with at least one race for juveniles almost every day. All of these are over the minimum trip of five furlongs. And although most of the two year old racing during April takes place at the lesser tracks, it doesn't stop trainers from introducing some of their better early types.

POINTERS

Keep an eye on where Brocklesby runners go, especially if they did well.

The majority of the April races are for maidens only (maidens are horses that have yet to win a race). However, there are also several "conditions" races which are open to winners of these early season two year old contests. Many are called 'novice races', they carry better prize money and previous winners get penalised for their success. For example, a Brocklesby winner might have to carry a 7lb penalty, which equates to a two length disadvantage against unpenalised rivals.

In addition to the type of race, the type of horse is important, and I go into more detail about this in Chapter 4. For now, it is worth pointing out that the bulk of the early juvenile winners tend to be smaller, stockier and more precocious. The punter able to get to the racetrack to pick them out will be at an advantage. However, many of them have little scope for future physical development, although better physical types do start to appear, especially at Newmarket's Craven meeting in mid-April. Two year old winners at this meeting invariably do well subsequently, as do many of the placed horses.

During April, the ground can often be soft or even heavy. This doesn't suit many horses and it demands considerable stamina. A horse's breeding will give some clues to its ability to act on a soft surface and see out the trip, but paddock inspection can also help. Horses with wide 'soup plate' feet cope better on soft going than those with neat 'donkey' feet since the former can spread their weight better. How a horse canters to the start can also give some clues to its ability to act on the surface. Animals with a 'daisy cutter' stride that skims the grass are better on a quicker surface whilst horses with a 'round' action that brings the knees up high do better on slower ground.

POINTERS

Establish whether the horse is suited to the going.

The only other thing to note about April is the abundance of sellers and claimers. The former requires the winner of the race to be offered for auction at the track immediately after the contest. The latter requires the owner of the horse to set a 'price' for the animal at which it can be claimed (purchased) after the race, regardless of its finishing position. The lower the price, the less weight it has to carry - a neat form of self-handicapping. These sellers and claimers serve a useful purpose, enabling trainers to get rid of their poorer animals or have a 'bit of a touch' (a gamble) with their slightly better two year olds.

May

May is important in three respects. Firstly, it tends to be the month when trainers introduce their better Ascot-bound juveniles, especially at the classier tracks such as Newbury and Newmarket although, as described above, one or two Royal Ascot two year old winners will have already shown themselves in April.

Secondly, the middle of May sees the start of the first six furlong races. This is an important development since it provides the slightly bigger, more stoutly bred (with stamina) early two year olds with winning opportunities. An extra furlong may not sound like a lot but it makes a significant difference for those juveniles with more stamina and less speed. Conversely, the extra 220 yards can prove an impossible task for the true sprinting speed merchants.

Thirdly, the month sees the introduction of the first 'black type' races for two year olds. These are 'listed' contests for fillies only at York (the Marygate Stakes) and Beverley (the Hilary Needler Trophy). These, and other 'black type races', are very important to owners. They entitle the winning and placed horses to list their achievements in any subsequent sales catalogue in value-enhancing 'black type' (emboldened lettering). This significantly increases their stud value, which will itself be significantly higher than the prize money they won.

There are two other races to note in May, namely the Lily Agnes Stakes over a sharp five furlongs at Chester and the National Stakes over a stiff five furlongs at Sandown. The first of these at Chester is a real test of the better early sprint juveniles and it takes some winning. In fact, the race is such a sprint from the start that it almost always favours those drawn closest to the rails. No horse drawn more than six stalls off the rail has won in the last 20 years – although it should be pointed out that horses initially drawn higher than sixth will be moved closer to the rail in the event that there are non runners from the lower drawn positions.

POINTERS

Look closely at the draw because, at some tracks, it makes a significant difference.

The second, the National Stakes requires a fair bit more stamina due to Sandown's stiff uphill climb but it still suits sprint specialists. Again, the draw can be very significant. The race is open to both colts and fillies and either can win. Winners usually head off to Royal Ascot for the Norfolk or Queen Mary Stakes and do well if they haven't had too hard a race.

June

The Royal Ascot juvenile races in late June dominate the agenda for most top trainers. It is possibly the most important shop window for trainers of two year olds. It also offers, of course, a massive value boost for the winning racehorses concerned, both in prize money and subsequent stud value. Winning a race at this meeting therefore also has extremely high kudos for owners.

The main two year old Royal meeting races are the Coventry Stakes, Queen Mary Stakes and Norfolk Stakes, all of which carry 'Group 2' status. Group races are a significant step up on listed contests and provide the winner as well as placed horses with considerable prestige with regard to future breeding value. They also carry considerably more prize money than the lesser contests.

On the maiden race front, the emphasis switches from five to six furlong races which dominate during the month, providing more opportunities for those juveniles that lack the blistering speed to win over five furlongs.

Other Ascot juvenile events of note include the Albany Stakes (Group 3), the Chesham Stakes (listed) and the Windsor Castle Stakes (listed). Other significant factors to note include the arrival of seven furlong races for juveniles in the middle of the month. This provides the first real stamina tests for the most stoutly bred types that might be expected to stay beyond a mile as three year olds.

It is some years since a two year old has won first time out at Royal Ascot (although *Kingsgate Native* came close in 2007). It is also almost impossible to win if the horse hasn't had at least a ten day break. Most Royal Ascot winners will therefore have completed their last race much earlier in the month.

July

July heralds the start of nurseries, which are handicaps exclusively for two year olds. The early nurseries are restricted to two year olds that have either won or been placed at least once in three earlier outings, a fact which gives the handicapper at least a small amount of form to go on, but they are notoriously difficult to predict. July is also important as the month in which the first 'Sales Races' appear. These high value two year old contests are restricted to horses that have been sold or bought in by their breeders as yearlings at public auction.

The Weatherbys Super Sprint was one of the first Sales Races to be established and is the first of the two year old season. It is particularly attractive to the owners of cheaper juveniles, since only those horses costing under £50,000 are eligible to run. Better still, the cheaper the horse, the less weight it has to carry - a sort of price-imposed handicapping system. The race carries a massive prize pot of over £140,000, and prize money is awarded down to tenth place – an unusual if not unwelcome consequence of the high cost of the entry fees. I personally won't be carping about this, though, since I co-owned the winner in 2004, with a speedy filly called *Siena Gold* who embodied many of the characteristics of typical winners of this race – inexpensive, an early type, competitive and well trained by Brian Meehan. Indeed, most winners of the Super Sprint tend to be listed class or better and come from the larger two year old training yards, Hannon's being the most successful in the race over recent years.

The other highly significant stepping stone for the better two year olds is the July meeting at Newmarket. This three day feast of racing held in early July includes several two year old 'Group' races, the Cherry Hinton, July Stakes and Superlative Stakes. Many of the winners here have already proved themselves at Royal Ascot and go on to win at the highest level the following year. There are also several other less valuable two year old races at the meeting that the top trainers use to introduce their better-class debutants. In particular, the Strutt & Parker Maiden Stakes over seven furlongs is a race worth noting as it is nearly always won by a classy individual.

One final race to bear in mind this month is the Princess Margaret Stakes at Ascot's King George meeting at the end of July; this fillies-only Group 3 attracts some very useful animals, most of whom have only been lightly raced by that point. However, as many winning and placed horses go on to win Group 1 races later in the season or during the following year, the outcome is well worth noting.

August

By August, the early precocious two year olds are beginning to struggle against the later maturing horses
of their own generation. Equally significant in terms
of their capability to win later in the season, horses
that have been on the go from March or early April
may start to become jaded, especially if they've had a
series of tough races in quick succession. From a betting point of view, this means that the early precocious,
compact horses are probably better avoided from August onwards, especially if they are competing against
the larger, later developing types that are now starting
to appear.

The highlights of the month are the two summer fes-
tivals at Glorious Goodwood and at the York Ebor
meeting. The former is a five day festival of high class
racing, including several Group contests for two year
olds as well as nurseries and high value maiden races.
The Group races attract many of the winning two year
olds from Royal Ascot and Newmarket's July meeting
but these horses don't have a good record of winning
at Goodwood. Both Ascot and Newmarket have stiff
uphill finishes, whilst Goodwood with its downhill finish is more suitable for speedy types.

It is nonetheless true that Goodwood's Group races
for two year olds take a lot of winning and the Vintage Stakes over seven furlongs is often won by horses
that go on to prove themselves in the Classics, such as
the 1,000 and 2,000 Guineas, at three. The two year
old Group races at York, later in the month, are even

tougher to win and invariably act as a springboard for subsequent Group I success. The best juvenile races at York are the Lowther Stakes for fillies and the Gimcrack for colts, both over six furlongs.

The Ebor meeting hosts one of the most valuable two year old races of the year: the St. Leger Yearling Stakes, worth over £300,000 in total prize money. This sales race is restricted to yearlings that were catalogued in the previous year's Doncaster Bloodstock St. Leger Yearling Sales. Only the top twenty performing horses get to compete, so there is no horse running just for the sake of the outing.

August provides one other important arrival, the start of one mile races for juveniles. Of course, a two year old that can win over a mile at the height of the summer will invariably be by a stallion that showed abundant stamina himself and more information about the importance of the stallion is provided in the next chapter.

September

The arrival of autumn brings a change in the maximum distance at which two year olds can race with the introduction in mid-September of races over nine and ten furlongs. However, the vast bulk of two year old racing is still over shorter distances and the maiden races at the better racecourses attract large fields of unexposed or unraced juveniles.

September also brings the first UK Group I race for two year olds only, the Fillies Mile at Ascot. This has been won over the years by some true champions and even the placed horses can go on to Classic success. Rather surprisingly, the Royal Lodge Stakes, an equivalent race for colts over one mile at the same meeting, attracts animals of lesser ability but it will occasionally produce a future champion and should not be underestimated.

During September, there are several other highly significant races for two year olds including the Mill Reef Stakes at Newbury and the May Hill, Flying Childers and Champagne Stakes, all at Doncaster.

It is also worth making a couple of observations about the maiden races in September and October. Firstly, they are used by trainers to give their more backward two year olds a bit of experience. Although such horses may have little real hope of winning, they can benefit from the opportunity to learn about racing and trainers can use these races in preparation for a more extensive three year old campaign.

Secondly, a small band of trainers will use the races to introduce a promising late developer who has the ability to win at two, but will also continue to develop and flourish at three. The betting market invariably knows which is which – meaning that for the trader or punter it is important to watch the market.

During the month, there is also an important amendment to the rules relating to nurseries. From mid-September onwards, juveniles who have been unplaced in all their runs to date, become eligible to run in these two year old handicaps, provided they've had three outings. This makes these races even tougher for the punter.

October

Although two year old racing continues right through to the end of the year, October is the most significant month in the season and is the one most eagerly awaited by form students. The key reason for this is that October contains three of the year's most prestigious races for juveniles: the Cheveley Park Stakes for fillies, the Dewhurst and the Racing Post Trophy for colts.

These Group 1 races are viewed as championship events each season and the outcomes are very significant for predictions about the winners and winter favourites for the following year's Classics like the Guineas, Oaks and Derby. But they are not the only important two year old races in October that have a bearing. Other important races this month include the Middle Park and Rockfel Stakes, both at Newmarket, and the Horris Hill Stakes at Newbury. For out and out sprinters there is also the Cornwallis Stakes at Ascot.

October is typically a month of change weather-wise and a cold start to autumn can affect horses since it will encourage growth of their winter coats which, in turn, can impact on their well-being. As described earlier, horses that have been in training all season may be feeling the effects of a long campaign. Known in racing parlance as being 'over the top' some will be beaten when you least expect it. At this time of the year, it is also worth remembering that fresher horses with relatively fewer miles on the clock do better – but a trip to the races and a paddock inspection is the only way of knowing.

CHAPTER 2

Breeding

BREEDING

A racehorse's breeding tells us a great deal about its chances of performing creditably as a two year old. Breeding is therefore of central importance to decisions relating to trading – whether a horse should be backed or layed. In this chapter I outline the main issues such as age, speed, stamina, precocity and gender, and I highlight the factors that will stand you in the strongest stead when backing or laying two year olds.

Several factors stand out when trying to assess the winning chances of a juvenile debutant and each can have a strong bearing on whether the horse should be backed or layed. But before we take a look at these in detail, it might be helpful to explain a little about the breeding process.

The breeding process

Each year, racehorse breeders with broodmares set out with the goal of having their mares 'covered' or mated with the most suitable stallion, at a price they can afford. If the mare has stamina they might be looking for a stallion with speed. If she has some weakness in conformation (her physical structure) then they might be looking for a sire to offset it. However, the ultimate aim is to breed a racehorse good enough to win races. This is because, if her foals are successful on the track, then her breeding value is increased and her bloodline enhanced.

Stallion owners need to ensure that their horse 'covers' the best mares available. This is because his progeny's success on the racecourse will influence the fee that can be charged for his 'service' in subsequent years. Top Coolmore stallions such as *Dylan Thomas* and *Duke of Marmalade* command fees of between £35,000 and £40,000 for a 'nomination' (the right to send a mare to be covered by one of them). At the lower end of the scale, an established two year old sire, such as *Bertolini*, will cost only £4,000, assuming a live foal eleven months later.

It is important to note that most breeders are breeding for the sales ring and one of two distinct markets. The first is precocious types that will win as two year olds, giving the purchaser a quick return. The second is for those aspiring to classic glory who will be best at three years old or older who are capable of giving their owners a long term return.

A stud farm operation such as Darley's will have top stallions to suit both types of breeder. For two year old success they have sires such as *Kheleyf* and *Exceed And Excel*, whilst for classic hopefuls there is *Manduro*, *Authorized*, and *New Approach*.

The 'covering' season in the Northern Hemisphere starts on February 14th and continues through to early June. The more popular stallions will mate with up to 150 mares during this four month period, covering some on several occasions in order to bring them into foal.

Foaling dates

The timing of the birth is everything for foals. This is because every racehorse is assumed to have the same birthday of January 1st regardless of the actual month of its birth. This means that a foal born before midnight on New Year's Eve is a walking disaster for the breeder. Such a foal would be classified as a yearling within a few hours or days of its birth and spend its whole flat racing career at an age disadvantage against the competition in its own generation. Equally worrying would be a foal with a June birth date since it will be physically far less mature than a foal born four or five months earlier.

As a consequence, breeders will do their utmost to ensure that foals are born at the most advantageous time and the following table (Table 1) illustrates this. It shows the percentage of foals (over 2000 in all) that passed through the sales ring in 2008. Around two thirds were born during March or earlier; a further quarter were born in April. By contrast, far fewer foals were born at the start of the year (January) and only seven per cent were born in May or June.

POINTERS

Early in the season, stick to backing two year olds that are actually two.

Table 1 : Foaling Dates of Yearlings sold in 2008

Month of birth	Number of horses	Percentage (%)
January	198	8
February	619	26
March	767	32
April	628	27
May	160	7
June	2	*
TOTAL	2,374	100%

It seems obvious that if a two year old is several months younger than its rivals then the age difference will be to its disadvantage, but this seems not to be reflected in the betting, despite the fact that the information is readily available in *The Racing Post.*

I have therefore explored the relationship further to make the point as clearly as possible and the results are illustrated in Table 2 below. Table 2 shows that age and winning potential are closely related at least as far as success at Royal Ascot is concerned. It contains data from all races at Royal Ascot over the ten years to 2008. It shows that early foals (born in January, February or March) have the highest chance of winning. Indeed, almost eighty per cent of all Royal Ascot winners were born in these three months.

These data show that even in June, the lack of physical maturity amongst many May-born two year olds counts against them. Most Royal Ascot winners tend to have been early foals and races such as the Coventry Stakes are invariably won by animals born in March or earlier. Not surprisingly May born foals have an appalling record here with about one winner every ten years (*Free Agent* in 2008 and *Tippett Boy* in 1997).

**Table 2: Success at Royal Ascot by month of birth
(56 races over the ten years between 1998 and 2008
(excluding results from the Royal Ascot meeting
staged at York in 2005)**

Actual Foaling Month	Success Rate at Royal Ascot
January	12 per cent
February	38 per cent
March	28 per cent
April	20 per cent
May	2 per cent

Royal Ascot is not the only event where the finding about date of birth appears to matter. Analyses of a wider spectrum of annual racing results show a similar effect – particularly in the early part of the juvenile season. I examined all the results of two year old racing in four recent seasons comparing win rate with month of birth. My analysis showed that around a third of all competing two year olds classified as 'late' (born in April, May or June) win less than one in ten of all juvenile races during the spring and early summer.

This means that backing May born two year olds during March, April and May is a very risky business. Although there are exceptions every year, the odds are against them and this is why, from a betting point of view, it has historically been much more lucrative to lay two year olds that have yet to reach their second birthday than to back them, since less than 10 per cent are successful.

The sire

Birthdays are not the only important influence on two year old success. Unsurprisingly, the sire makes a significant contribution to the juvenile's ability to compete effectively with its peers as a two year old. But what are the important factors? Is it speed or stamina in the sire that matters most?

It is certainly true that the top sires of two year olds, in terms of number of juvenile winners in a season, tend to have been speed merchants themselves. Table 3 illustrates this point. It shows the high percentage strike rate for the progeny of stallions that were themselves sprinters, excelling over distances of less than a mile.

Table 3: Top sires of two year olds (by winners) in 2008

Stallion (best trip)	Proportion of winners to runners amongst 2 year old progeny	Strike rate (per cent win) %
Oasis Dream (sprint winner)	32-61	52
Kheleyf (winner over 7 furlongs)	27-57	47
Danehill Dancer (sprint winner)	25-63	40
Bahamian Bounty (sprint winner)	24-51	47

Kyllachy (sprint winner)	24-70	34
Captain Rio (sprint winner)	22-62	35
Invincible Spirit (sprint winner)	21-52	40
Exceed and Excel (sprint winner)	21-60	35
Royal Applause (sprint winner)	20-58	34
Noverre (winner over a mile)	18-39	46

This Table lists last year's (2008) top ten stallions – that is, the stallions that sired the greatest number of two year old winners. All bar one were at their personal best over distances of less than a mile and all of them won races themselves as two year olds. This means that speedy precocious stallions capable of winning in their juvenile year tend to give their progeny an important advantage.

Of course, that's not to say that there aren't some exceptions. For example, a number of more stoutly bred sires do get two year old winners and *Galileo* and *Montjeu* are excellent illustrations, but their progeny tend not to do well over the sprint distances of five or six furlongs.

POINTERS

Look out for the stallion's own success at two.

The importance of the stallion in this regard is further emphasised by taking a look at the stallions that have produced excellent three year olds. Table 4 lists seven stallions that have a good record of getting horses that do well at three. The Table shows, by contrast with the figures in Table 3, that their progeny do less well at two. It seems that whilst these stallions produce excellent three year olds and older animals, they are not capable of siring so many horses precocious enough to win at two.

Table 4: Other sires of two year olds (by winners) 2008

	Proportion of winners to runners amongst 2 year old progeny	Strike rate (per cent win) %
King's Best	10-45	22
Dr Fong	9-45	20
Rock of Gibraltar	7-40	18
Alhaarth	5-38	13
Selkirk	2-34	6
Medicean	6-24	25
Green Desert	2-21	10

I use the above examples merely as an illustration of the importance of a stallion in his progeny's ability to succeed as a juvenile. Each year, these statistics change as new stallions arrive and older ones retire, but a large core remain and knowledge of their ability to get two year old winners can be very significant when betting on juveniles.

Another useful aid to finding a winner is *The Racing Post's* stamina index for sires. Although most of us will remember the racecourse exploits of the top stallions, it doesn't always follow that their progeny show similar stamina traits. *The Racing Post* data helpfully reflect the average winning race distance of a particular sire's progeny.

POINTERS

Consider the importance of the stallion's stamina index when deciding if a juvenile will be suited by the trip.

This point is illustrated in the following Table (Table 5). The horses listed here are the successful sires of two year olds that appear in Table 3. It shows that all of them, with the exception of *Danehill Dancer*, have a stamina index of below 8.0 furlongs. Put another way, they are sprinters rather than stayers and it appears that they pass this ability on to a significant number of their foals.

Table 5: Stamina indices for the 10 most successful sires of two year old winners in 2008

Stallion	Stamina index in furlongs
Oasis Dream	7.3
Kheleyf	Too soon to assess
Danehill Dancer	8.0
Bahamian Bounty	6.6
Kyllachy	6.3
Captain Rio	6.5
Invincible Spirit	7.6
Exceed and Excel	Too soon to assess
Royal Applause	7.6
Noverre	7.9

By contrast, the majority of the stallions with a less positive winner to runner ratio for their two year old progeny, have a much higher stamina index (see Table 6).

Table 6: Stamina indices for 10 less successful sires of two year old winners in 2008

Stalllion	Stamina index in furlongs
King's Best	8.5
Dr Fong	9.6
Rock of Gibraltar	8.9
Alhaarth	10.2
Selkirk	8.8
Medicean	8.7
Green Desert	7.8

The stamina trait also has a bearing on the type of two year old that wins at different tracks. Although I go into more detail about the importance of the race-course itself in Chapter 4, it is worth pointing out here that stamina and track interact with one another. Furthermore, the sire's stamina or lack of it is not the only trait that can be passed on to his foals. Some stallions can also be an important influence on their progeny's preference for soft or fast ground.

Although some horses are happy to race on any surface, more often than not, an animal that likes to hear its hooves 'rattle' on firm going is nowhere near as comfortable on a soft surface. Likewise, few racehorses that relish heavy ground are as happy on ground that is rock hard.

POINTERS

Take account of the stallion's preference for the ground.

The preferences that a horse can display for one type of ground over another can be caused by a variety of factors, including the animal's build. However, breeding plays a significant part. This makes it an important consideration when backing or laying debutants and lightly raced juveniles.

Some sires get winners on all types of racing surface, whilst others tend to have a better strike rate on faster or slower ground. Listed below in Table 7 are the top

40 stallions in 2008 (based on the number of two year old winners they sired). I explored the pattern of winning and losing two year olds for a period up to two years to 2008. I looked at who won, and I looked at the state of the ground. In some cases, a clear pattern emerged. Some sires, such as *Captain Rio* and *One Cool Cat* appear to get progeny that do well on soft ground. Others, such as *Invincible Spirit* get two year olds that prefer the going to be faster. But caution is required if you plan to use these data for betting purposes. Some racehorses will win on ground they detest – it is as if their courage gets them home.

To make matters worse, historically some racecourses haven't always been particularly honest about the ground conditions reported to newspapers since extremes can deter trainers, leaving the track with few runners and even fewer paying customers.

Table 7: The top 40 sires of two year old winners in 2008 and a summary of the 'going' preferences of their progeny

SIRE	SUMMARY OF GOING PREFERENCES SHOWN BY PROGENY
Oasis Dream	Act on most except very firm
Kheleyf	Act well on fast but poor on soft
Danehill Dancer	Act on all but better on good or softer
Bahamian Bounty	Act on all
Kyllachy	Better on fast but act on all
Captain Rio	Better on a softer surface and fibresand
Invincible Spirit	Slight preference for faster ground
Exceed and Excel	Act on most except heavy
Royal Applause	Act on all
Noverre	Act on most except heavy
One Cool Cat	Better on soft and poor on firm
Galileo	Act on all
Diktat	Act on most except firm
Verglas	Better on good or softer
Dubai Destination	Act on all
Montjeu	Act on all
Pivotal	Better on softer surface but can win on firm
Acclamation	Act on all
Dansili	Act on all but best on firm
Bertolini	Act on all
Danetime	Act on most except very firm
Haafhd	Act well on polytrack
Refuse to Bend	Better on good or softer, poor on firm
Fasliyev	Act on all
Namid	Act on most except heavy
Elusive City	Better on fast but poor on heavy
Red Ransom	Act on most except heavy
Tobougg	Act on all
Monsieur Bond	Difficult to assess due to too little data
Johannesburg	Act on all
Giant's Causeway	Act on all
Choisir	Act on most except very firm
Cape Cross	Act on most but poor on heavy
King's Best	Act on all
Elusive Quality	Act on most except heavy
Daylami	Act on most but better on good or faster
Compton Place	Act on all
Dr. Fong	Act on most but poor on heavy
Beat Hollow	Act best on good or softer but OK on fast
Pyrus	Difficult to assess due to too little data

It would also seem that some sires have an influence on their progeny's ability to win first time out. I do think this finding is slightly surprising but I have listed the best and worst sires from the top 40 for reference. Sires whose progeny win first time out on more than 10 per cent of occasions are *Oasis Dream, Montjeu, Pivotal, Acclamation* and *Elusive Quality*. Sires whose progeny win first time out on fewer than five per cent of occasions are *Captain Rio, Bertolini, Tobougg* and *Compton Place*.

The dam

Understanding a sire's credentials can help us find two year old winners and losers but the dam can also shed some important light on the juvenile debutant's chances.

Obviously, there are very many more brood mares than there are stallions since only the best colts go on to become sires. But in much the same way as is true for the stallions, the dam's ability, if she ever raced, is important. It can tell us a great deal about the chances of an unraced juvenile winning at two.

An analysis of the top 100 two year olds of 2008 (based on the ratings published in *The Racing Post*) is most revealing. More than 80 per cent of them – and they were highly successful runners - had a dam that had either won at two or bred foals that had gone on to be placed at two. Furthermore, in many instances, both these significant signposts were present for all to see in the juvenile's pedigree.

POINTERS

Don't ignore the dam's ability as a two year old or her progeny's success at two.

The implications for the punter are clear. The dam's early maturity or her progeny's precocious ability follows through the bloodline, even if the sire is not known to get two year old winners. *Rainbow Quest*, the sire of *Crowded House*, the top rated UK two year old of 2008, is a good example of this. *Rainbow Quest* is not noted for getting precocious two year olds, but the dam of *Crowded House* is, so it looks as if speed somewhere in the family is key.

CHAPTER 3

Training

TRAINING

As we've seen, a racehorse's breeding will have a significant bearing on its chances of winning at two but so will the trainer to whom it's been entrusted. In this chapter, I outline some of the issues about the trainers and their yards that the serious punter should know.

The leading trainers

Perhaps the first and most important point to make about trainers of two year olds, is that there are relatively few trainers who really excel at this challenge. In 2008, for example, over 300 UK trainers ran two year olds during the flat turf season. However, 19 of them won more than half of all two year old races. In fact, a little over 60 per cent of two year old races were won by just 29 trainers. Table 8 illustrates this clearly. It shows Richard Hannon at the top of the table in 2008 with almost twice as many two year old winners as his nearest rival that year, Mark Johnston.

Table 8 : Trainers and two year old winners on the turf in 2008

TRAINER	NUMBER OF TWO YEAR OLD WINS
Richard Hannon	93
Mark Johnston	48
Mick Channon	41
Bryan Smart	31
Kevin Ryan	31
John Gosden	27
Barry Hills	26
Brian Meehan	25
Michael Jarvis	23
Richard Fahey	23
Paul Cole	23
Sir Michael Stoute	19
Jeremy Noseda	19
Saeed Bin Suroor	18
Karl Burke	18
Michael Bell	18
William Haggas	16
David Evans	16
Ralph Beckett	15
TOTAL	530

Of course, the fact that some trainers are clearly very good at training two year olds, and some have developed specialist skills in relation to two year olds, doesn't mean that the other trainers lack ability. A combination of factors are important, including knowledge, ability, strategy and tactics. There is also the fact that the majority of the more precocious yearlings are sent to the trainers with the best record. For the punter, it is worth understanding a bit more about what these records can tell us.

It is also true that every year, relative newcomers to the training ranks start to make their mark and in 2008 a name that caught many people's eye was Tom Dascombe. To date he has trained only 29 two year old winners, but he started so recently (in 2006) that his success in prize money terms must be noted. For example, in 2008, he made headlines by winning two Group 2 juvenile races, the July Stakes and the Super-lative Stakes at Newmarket, in the space of two days. Further success in the juvenile department looks on the cards in 2009 since he has significantly increased his string for the coming season.

POINTERS

Check out runners from the top two year old trainers and keep an eye on their newcomers.

The training process

First of all, it may be helpful to understand the training process. It begins at annual yearling sales, at various locations, that start in August and run through until early December. In the following spring, further unraced animals are sold at 'breeze-up' sales when they are galloped over a short distance prior to auction. The yearlings are sold unbroken, so the first task facing the trainers is to get a saddle on them. In some instances, the breaking process, as it is known, is undertaken at the trainer's establishment but there are also specialists who undertake the job of getting the horse ready to be ridden.

Some yearlings are easier than others but, typically the job takes between ten days and a month from start to finish. The experts like to take time to teach the animal about being ridden and to spend more time at this early stage, arguing that it is helpful from a learning point of view. But some trainers take a harder line, arguing 'a horse doesn't need to learn dressage to go fast in a straight line.'

Once an animal can be ridden, then the training process can begin in earnest. To start with, young horses need to get used to trotting and cantering, latterly in small groups so they feel familiar with other horses around them. Those that cope best with these early rigours will then start galloping over short distances with horses of similar ability.

The exact timing of this development work will vary from trainer to trainer but those with large strings of two year olds (50 or more) will be getting going with the more precocious types soon after the turn of the year.

That makes it sound easy but it certainly isn't. Some yearlings and two year olds flourish on such a routine but others don't cope at all. They need to be given more time to mature mentally and physically. Other things can also go wrong: young horses get sore shins from over exerting still developing limbs, whilst others can become weak as they continue to grow or lose weight if the training process becomes too stressful.

Trainers need to give these horses more time, cutting back on serious work and this may delay their first run on a racecourse. The animal's temperament can also have a bearing on its ability to cope in these early months of fitness development.

By mid-March, the top trainers of two year olds will have sorted out their early types from their late maturers and will be starting serious work with the better early ones in readiness for the start of the turf season.

Some trainers will conduct trial gallops in order to sort out a pecking order of ability. Others just have an eye for it. Either way, this performance knowledge isn't lost on stable staff or owners and it's not long before the bookies know as well. However, what happens on the gallops at home doesn't always translate pound for pound onto the racecourse. For starters, some two year olds who do well at home just don't cope with the racecourse experience. Possibly, the crowd, the course or the change of scenery put them off. Others show little ability when working on the gallops, but the penny drops when they get to the track. It is also worth pointing out that, more often than not, the unexpected poor performance of a horse can be best explained by illness or injury.

The temperament of the horse

There appears to be a relationship between temperament and winning. Some racehorses just want to lead the pack and dominate their peers. *George*

Washington is an excellent example of an alpha male with strong temperament as well as a strong desire to win. In his case, as with so many of the great horses, his assertive manner and quirky behaviour are both aspects of his capability on the track. Others are followers of the pack, rather than leaders, appearing content to stay out of trouble near the back of the field. This is a difficult dimension for the punter to assess, but is worth a thought at the racetrack when it is possible to look at the horses in the paddock and pre-parade ring. Some two year olds may be fractious or hard to manage, whilst others are whinnying noisily – an alarm call to mum – a sure sign of mental immaturity.

Temperament when it is focused positively is no bad thing, and this is true for fillies as well as colts and geldings. *Siena Gold*, whom I mentioned in Chapter 1, a winner of the Super Sprint, had temperament in spades, sometimes making it difficult for some of her handlers to enter her box to saddle her, but it didn't stop her from winning three races at two.

POINTERS

Check if you can, on the temperament of the horse. Behaviour in the paddock and pre-parade ring can give you a clue.

Of course, temperament or an aggressive or iron will as it might manifest in some juveniles is not always a good thing. It can impact on a two year old's ability to learn, its desire to win and, in the case of fillies, it is not easy to change. With a colt at least, it is possible to geld (castrate) him, thereby reducing his levels of testosterone, making him more manageable and more easy to train. Gelding, it is argued, whilst some owners are very sensitive about it, tends to make a difficult horse much easier to manage and it helps him focus his mind on racing.

Of course the older the horse is at the point when gelding is undertaken, the longer the recovery time. For this reason, I've tended to geld any cheap yearling colts I've bought as soon as possible - their pedigrees are never going to make them future sires.

Training to win first time out

Knowing the first time out strike rates of the top two year old yards is important when backing or laying juveniles and this information is readily to hand each day on the Signpost page of *The Racing Post* and on their website.

Trainers employ different strategies with regard to debutants – first timers – and, as a consequence, their readiness to win at the first time of asking varies. For example, the two year old newcomers from Saeed Bin Suroor's yard are almost always primed for victory on their first appearance. Of 250 juveniles sent out by the stable in recent years for their first ever run, 54 won, a success rate of 22 per cent. Likewise, Jeremy Noseda appears to have his two year olds ready to do themselves justice on their first outing. He has a record of 36 winners from 229 horses (16 per cent).

By contrast, some top two year old trainers, such as Brian Meehan (first time strike rate 6 per cent) and Tim Easterby (first time strike rate 4 per cent) appear to take the view that a horse's first day on the racecourse should be as stress free as possible in order to maximise the long term positive benefits of the learning. In the case of Brian Meehan, for example, *David Junior* (Champion Stakes, Dubai Duty Free Stakes and Eclipse Stakes winner) was third on his first outing at 5/2, *Red Rocks* (Breeders Cup Turf and Man O' War Stakes winner) was 9th at 50/1 and *Crowded House* (Racing Post Trophy winner) was 10th at 25/1.

POINTERS

Check the trainer's first time strike rate.

Other trainers of two year olds have even lower strike rates first time out. For example, both Milton Bradley and Mark Brisbourne have sent out over 50 debutant two year olds in recent years and yet none of them has won first time out.

Of course, saying that horses from particular yards tend not to win first time out, is not the same as saying that they aren't trying. It just means that they might still have a few lessons to learn, such as breaking fast from the starting gate. For the punter, however, the implication is that first-time out winners from these yards achieve their success through raw ability. They are often very smart individuals in the making and worth following.

Table 9 below shows the individual strike rates for the top 30 UK trainers of two year olds, based on their performances over the past nine years. The chart also sets out the profit or loss that results by blindly backing each debutant from individual stables.

Not only do these statistics show the varying approaches taken by different yards with regard to their debutants, it also shows that it is a risky business backing beginners. Even the most successful training establishments vary. Of the 30 trainers listed, only six provided a profitable return from backing first timers. For example, almost a third of Saeed Bin Suroor's first timers started at even money or shorter, so you would still make a loss despite his excellent strike rate.

POINTERS

Be very careful backing two year old debutants. You might consider laying some of them instead.

Table 9: Debutants' success rates 2000 - 2008

TRAINER	SUCCESS RATE %	PROFIT OR LOSS BACKING ALL
Richard Hannon	10	-£254
Mark Johnston	13	-£39
Mick Channon	9	-£278
Bryan Smart	9	-£65
Kevin Ryan	10	-£60
John Gosden	11	-£36
Barry Hills	8	-£187
Brian Meehan	6	-£185
Michael Jarvis	12	-£43
Richard Fahey	8	+£30
Paul Cole	13	-£61
Sir Michael Stoute	15	-£75
Jeremy Noseda	16	+£5
Saeed Bin Suroor	22	-£29
Karl Burke	5	-£56
Michael Bell	7	-£162
William Haggas	6	-£105
David Evans	8	+£49
Ralph Beckett	9	+£9
Amanda Perrett	5	-£153
Ed Dunlop	6	-£209
Henry Cecil	18	-£25
Ed McMahon	13	+£53
Tim Easterby	4	-£244
Sylvester Kirk	5	-£101
Sir Mark Prescott	8	-£114
Simon Callaghan	0	-£23
Peter Winkworth	10	+£114
Peter Chapple-Hyam	10	-£77
Roger Charlton	8	-£112

If backing Saeed Bin Suroor's newcomers blindly is definitely a losing business, it is also true that there's more profit to be had from laying the debutants from some of the bigger yards such as Hannon's and Channon's. This is because around 90 per cent of them get turned over. A £1 bet on each of their debutants over the past eight years would have lost you more than £500.

The strike rate at particular tracks

I tend to avoid any yard with a first time strike rate of less than 5 per cent for its juvenile newcomers. But this percentage represents the trainer's average success rate across all UK race tracks. It is therefore worth looking at the yard's strike rate at particular tracks because some trainers have favourites and the probability of their winning there is often raised. The information the punter needs to determine this is also set out in *The Racing Post*.

Mark Johnston and Richard Hannon, both of whom have trained nearly 100 debutant winners since 2000 provide good illustrations of this point. Each has racecourse preferences for their better two year olds and, conversely, there are tracks where their winners are few and far between.

For example, Mark Johnston sends more juvenile debutants to Hamilton than any other racecourse. He has an 18 per cent winner strike rate there. Furthermore, 60 per cent of his two year old debutants at this racecourse in recent years have finished in the first three.

Johnston doesn't send too many juveniles down south for their first outings but those that have made the trip to Brighton, Epsom and Folkestone have rarely gone home empty handed.

By contrast, in the past eight years, he has had only one winner at Haydock and of 31 debutants at this track, over 60 per cent were unplaced. His debutants at Bath, Newbury and Yarmouth are also more often than not out of the money.

Hannon also has tracks he favours for possible first-time winners. For example, his runners at Leicester only win on 3 per cent of occasions. He also rarely introduces horses up north but those that make the journey to York have finished in the first three in nearly 70 per cent of races. Newbury is his course of choice numerically, but only 6 per cent of his horses are good enough to win at the first time of asking and just over 20 per cent finish in the first three. However, Folkestone is where Richard Hannon's debutants must be feared most. His yard has an astonishing 25 per cent strike rate there.

POINTERS

Note the trainer's record at the track for two year olds first time out.

Table 10 sets out the tracks to note for seven UK top trainers. It shows the percentage win and placing rate for each trainer at 37 tracks.

Table 10: Tracks to note for trainers (win % / placed %)
(Assumes 5 or more runners at the track)

	Hannon	Johnston	Channon	Stoute	Gosden	Hills	Meehan
Ascot	13/21	6/47	13/53	11/33	0/18	18/27	9/18
Ayr	---	19/40	---	---	---	---	---
Bath	18/35	0/14	6/32	---	0/20	10/50	8/33
Beverley	---	21/61	---	---	---	---	---
Brighton	0/50	40/60	0/36	---	---	---	---
Carlisle	---	33/58	---	---	---	---	---
Catterick	---	15/50	---	---	---	---	---
Chepstow	19/31	20/40	5/5	---	---	---	0/13
Chester	---	0/33	---	---	---	---	---
Doncaster	14/43	10/24	6/24	12/24	19/45	7/35	0/40
Epsom	---	50/83	---	---	---	---	---
Folkestone	25/38	---	8/54	---	---	---	---
Goodwood	8/41	8/25	8/33	---	10/29	9/31	5/21
Hamilton	---	18/60	40/60	---	---	---	---
Haydock	6/41	3/39	6/35	---	15/54	14/41	6/18
Kempton	14/38	20/30	0/33	0/13	33/47	11/22	0/10
Leicester	3/28	15/33	14/43	16/46	12/27	5/50	7/21
Lingfield (Turf)	16/37	---	8/31	10/20	---	---	0/0
Lingfield (A/W)	14/41	19/25	19/38	5/33	8/41	7/21	11/41
Musselburgh	---	4/21	---	---	---	---	---
Newbury	6/21	---	8/19	14/46	6/25	7/24	6/23
Newcastle	---	14/42	10/40	---	---	---	---
Newmarket (Rowley)	12/36	8/15	9/39	10/23	16/27	9/28	9/30
Newmarket (July)	11/32	13/25	3/9	15/36	13/45	8/25	6/33
Nottingham	0/27	14/28	10/24	22/43	0/7	0/33	7/33
Pontefract	---	5/26	---	---	---	0/40	---
Redcar	---	10/37	9/45	---	0/33	---	---
Ripon	---	12/48	29/43	---	---	---	---
Salisbury	5/25	---	9/28	0/30	8/28	0/31	15/31
Sandown	14/31	16/37	9/36	17/47	12/29	6/47	0/15

Southwell (A/W)	---	14/29	---	---	---	---	---
Thirsk	---	18/46	11/44	---	---	---	---
Warwick	9/27	8/38	4/33	27/45	---	0/50	7/29
Windsor	10/30	---	8/24	18/36	---	14/30	4/14
Wolverhampton	0/0	12/23	0/17	17/58	0/29	---	11/33
Yarmouth	---	0/24	15/23	23/43	9/41	0/40	10/10
York	11/67	15/41	13/60	---	---	5/32	---

Table 11 contains information about the other more notable trainers of two year olds, and their obvious course preferences to help you when backing or laying debutants.

Table 11: The course preferences of other notable trainers

TRAINER		DEBUTANT TRACK RECORD (+ = positive record. − = negative record)
Michael Bell	+	Folkestone, Hamilton, Haydock, Musselburgh, Yarmouth.
	−	Lingfield, Newcastle, Nottingham, Sandown, Thirsk, Warwick, Windsor, Wolverhampton.
Karl Burke	+	Carlisle, Catterick, Haydock, Musselburgh, Nottingham, Ripon, Yarmouth.
	−	Beverley, Hamilton, Newcastle, Pontefract, Redcar, Southwell, Thirsk, Windsor, York.

Peter Chapple-Hyam	+	Leicester, Newmarket (July), Windsor, Yarmouth.
	–	Goodwood, Lingfield (A/W), Warwick.
Roger Charlton	+	Haydock, Lingfield (Turf), Nottingham, Windsor, Wolverhampton.
	–	Doncaster, Goodwood, Kempton, Leicester, Lingfield (A/W), Newmarket (Rowley), Salisbury.
Paul Cole	+	Doncaster, Kempton, Newmarket (Rowley), Wolverhampton, York.
	–	Goodwood, Newbury, Nottingham, Salisbury, Warwick, Windsor.
Tim Easterby	+	Catterick, Pontefract, Ripon, Southwell, Thirsk.
	–	Beverley, Carlisle, Doncaster, Haydock, Newcastle, Nottingham, Redcar.
Richard Fahey	+	Beverley, Doncaster, Hamilton, Haydock, Musselburgh, Newcastle, Southwell.
	–	Carlisle, Catterick, Chester, Nottingham, Redcar, Thirsk, Wolverhampton, York.
William Haggas	+	Haydock, Leicester, Pontefract, Salisbury, Yarmouth.
	–	Ascot, Kempton, Lingfield, Newmarket (Rowley), Newmarket (July), Nottingham, Ripon, Warwick, Windsor, Wolverhampton.
Michael Jarvis	+	Doncaster, Goodwood, Kempton, Lingfield (A/W), Newbury, Nottingham, York.
	–	Leicester, Newmarket (Rowley), Newmarket (July), Sandown, Windsor.

Jeremy Noseda	+	Ascot, Leicester, Lingfield (Turf), Lingfield (A/W).
	–	Doncaster, Goodwood, Haydock, Kempton, Newbury, Newmarket (Rowley), Windsor, Yarmouth.
Kevin Ryan	+	Ayr, Beverley, Catterick, Chester, Hamilton, Haydock, Leicester, Newcastle, Newmarket (Rowley), York.
	–	Carlisle, Doncaster, Nottingham, Pontefract, Redcar, Ripon, Southwell, Wolverhampton.
Saeed Bin Suroor	+	Doncaster, Lingfield (A/W), Newbury, Newcastle, Salisbury, Warwick.
	–	Goodwood, Leicester, Lingfield (Turf), Newmarket (Rowley), Sandown, Windsor, York.
Bryan Smart	+	Beverley, Hamilton, Musselburgh, Newcastle, Ripon.
	–	Ayr, Bath, Carlisle, Catterick, Haydock, Pontefract, Warwick, Windsor, Wolverhampton, York.
Marcus Tregoning	+	Leicester, Lingfield (A/W).
	–	Chepstow, Doncaster, Kempton, Newmarket (Rowley), Salisbury, Windsor.

What the odds can tell you

Money normally talks in the betting ring when these bigger two year old training establishments have runners, since the stable will often have very reliable yardsticks from which to measure a debutant's ability. However, it is not all plain sailing if you are a punter that likes to back favourites.

During the past eight years, Mark Johnston has introduced 10 juveniles that started at evens or shorter and half were beaten. Richard Hannon has had five odds-on shots over the same period and three were beaten. Mick Channon has done slightly better with four out of seven winning and Brian Meehan has scored with three out of four that went to post as odds-on debutants. Noseda has won with six out of eight, John Gosden has scored with three out of five and Sir Michael Stoute has delivered 13 out of 22 but Saeed Bin Suroor has seen only eight out of eighteen odds-on shots hit the target. As some of these losers have been as short as 4/11, it's a brave person who backs them.

It is worth remembering that although a trainer might know which is the best two year old in his own yard, he won't have raced his newcomer against the opposition. He can therefore only make a calculated guess as to the merits of the other runners. Obviously, a trainer can telephone his rivals, but there's no obligation on their part to give information away.

POINTERS

Backing short priced newcomers is a risky strategy.

Despite this, the betting ring is cautious about new-comers from the top yards. In the case of the Johnston stable, around 10 per cent of debutants in the last five years started in double figures. He had one winner at 28/1, but 60 per cent of his winners started at 5/1 or less. Hannon's runners were equally poor value with around 50 per cent of the debutant winners starting at 5/1 or lower. Hannon has had the occasional outsider that surprises – he's had two 25/1 shots and a 33/1 winner in recent years. A similar picture is also true for Mick Channon and John Gosden. For example, around 70 per cent of Channon's and most of Gosden's fancied newcomers started at 5/1 or less. However, Channon also had a 25/1 and a 50/1 winner, as did Gosden, confirming that not all results are expected.

Saeed Bin Suroor's runners represent particularly poor value to the punter trying to find a first time out winner. Over 90 per cent of his winning debutants over the past five years started at 5/1 or less. The Godolphin yard might not be a gambling stable but information reaches the bookies about the horses' chances since no newcomer has won at more than 10/1 in the last eight years.

The pattern of short prices for the fancied debutants trained by the most successful trainers is evident over and over again. For example, it is true for Sir Michael Stoute (60 per cent priced at 5/1 or less), William Haggas (64 per cent), Kevin Ryan (53 per cent), Michael Jarvis (51 per cent) and Bryan Smart (50 per cent). But the trainer with the most short-priced winners is Jeremy Noseda with 80 per cent at 5/1 or less. Luckily for some, even he has had a 33/1 newcomer surprise the betting ring with a win at Newbury in 2008. Scant few start at this sort of price out of his yard and go on to victory.

Finding winners second time out

An important fact about the average two year old is that he/she is thought to improve by 5lbs (in terms of ability) between the first and second run. An equally important fact about the top two year old yards is that if they didn't win with their juveniles first-time out, then there's a greater likelihood that they will win at the second time of asking. Saeed Bin Suroor has the best strike rate for his second time out maidens. Of these, 35 per cent in the past eight years have won, providing a level stake profit of £32 (to £1).

Sir Michael Stoute has also achieved an impressive second time strike rate with 26 per cent of winners to runners, whilst John Gosden has scored with a quarter of his. In fact, eighteen of the top nineteen two year old trainers of 2008 improved significantly on their debutant strike rate at the second time of asking. The only exception was David Evans who equalled his debutant score. Table 12 illustrates this clearly, and it shows the percentage strike rate for the top trainers for their juveniles on a second outing. It also shows the degree of profit or loss from backing them all.

Table 12 : Strike rate second time out: trainers and the overall profit and loss

TRAINER	SECOND TIME SUCCESS RATE 2000-2008 %	PROFIT OR LOSS BACKING ALL
Richard Hannon	17	-£76
Mark Johnston	20	-£39
Mick Channon	16	-£109
Bryan Smart	12	-£32
Kevin Ryan	15	-£30
John Gosden	25	+£3
Barry Hills	20	-£73
Brian Meehan	16	-£132
Michael Jarvis	20	-£7
Richard Fahey	10	-£16
Paul Cole	16	-£80
Sir Michael Stoute	26	-£38
Jeremy Noseda	23	-£44
Saeed Bin Suroor	35	+£32
Karl Burke	17	+£63
Michael Bell	17	-£51
William Haggas	18	-£24
David Evans	8	-£96
Ralph Beckett	14	+£28

What Table 12 shows very clearly is that, as with debutants, punters would have made an overall loss had they backed all the second time out maidens. No surprises here, perhaps. But it is interesting that their losses would been much smaller, suggesting a better strike rate. Some punters hold the view that two year olds that finish second on their first outing will often disappoint in their next race. However, the statistics don't bear this theory out. An examination of the facts for the past nine years shows that juveniles finishing second first time out won their next race on nearly a third of occasions. By comparison, horses that finished third in their first race only went on to win next time on 20 per cent of occasions.

POINTERS

Backing juveniles from the top two year old yards second time out is less risky than backing debutants.

Trainers preferences for courses second time out

As with trainers sending their juveniles out for the first time, it's clear is that most have racecourse preferences when they're keen to get the 'job done' on the juvenile's second outing. For example, around a third of all Richard Hannon's 'second time out' maidens win when they are sent to Brighton, Doncaster and York (a different pattern than is true for his debutants) but he has a much poorer strike rate at Ascot and Folkestone (where, in the latter case, his debutants do very well).

Mark Johnston doesn't expect to come back empty handed from Ayr (40 per cent strike rate) or Sandown (54 per cent) but he doesn't do well at Epsom, Lingfield (A/W) or the Newmarket July Course.

Mick Channon is another who likes to score when he sends them North of the Border where he has second time out strike rates of 29 per cent at Ayr, 33 per cent at Musselburgh and 29 per cent at Hamilton. His best track is Beverley where 46 per cent have hit the target in recent years.

Of the others, Stoute does particularly well at Salisbury and Yarmouth and John Gosden has an excellent record at Haydock and Newmarket's July Course. Barry Hills has an outstanding record at Chester (60 per cent), a favourite for him, and Brian Meehan rarely sends them to Newmarket at the second time of asking without strong hopes of victory. Table 13 shows the pattern of preference for particular tracks for seven leading UK trainers.

POINTERS

Look at trainers' preferences for tracks for a second outing – they aren't necessarily the same as their preferences for those running for the first time.

Table 13: Tracks to note for second time out maidens (win %)

(Assumes 5 or more runners at the track)

*Means less than 5 second time maiden runners

	Hannon	Johnston	Channon	Stoute	Gosden	Hills	Meehan
Ascot	9	17	8	29	0	20	8
Ayr	*	40	29	*	*	27	*
Bath	21	0	16	*	*	7	21
Beverley	*	10	46	0	*	*	*
Brighton	30	33	14	---	*	*	13
Carlisle	---	30	*	---	---	---	---
Catterick	---	24	*	*	---	*	---
Chepstow	14	14	5	*	14	*	*
Chester	17	25	*	*	*	60	*
Doncaster	29	20	9	25	31	24	*
Epsom	22	0	17	*	*	40	*
Folkestone	9	*	26	*	*	*	13
Goodwood	11	33	10	*	23	20	10
Hamilton	*	26	29	---	---	*	---
Haydock	19	5	30	*	40	27	17
Kempton	11	*	22	43	14	46	36
Leicester	24	23	11	24	21	17	16
Lingfield (Turf)	15	---	15	*	*	25	17
Lingfield (A/W)	16	0	19	16	18	25	17
Musselburgh	---	11	33	---	---	*	---
Newbury	12	14	10	20	35	11	19
Newcastle	---	16	30	---	---	*	---
Newmarket (Rowley)	21	11	23	29	26	13	38
Newmarket (July)	23	0	11	17	41	11	60
Nottingham	27	16	20	15	11	10	13
Pontefract	50	22	0	*	*	33	*
Redcar	*	19	29	33	*	0	---
Ripon	*	24	10	---	---	*	*
Salisbury	18	---	11	50	27	44	19
Sandown	21	54	18	25	0	25	7

Southwell (A/W)	---	9	*	---	*	*	50
Thirsk	*	18	11	*	---	*	20
Warwick	23	11	15	0	---	6	33
Windsor	15	*	12	17	*	13	13
Wolverhampton	13	19	25	17	14	13	8
Yarmouth	14	13	15	47	31	*	25
York	30	17	12	*	*	12	0

Perhaps unsurprisingly, the above trainers aren't the only ones to seek out specific tracks for their 'second time out' stars, and for those with less obvious chances. Table 14 shows the pattern of their preferences.

Table 14: Other trainers and their preferences for particular tracks

TRAINER		SECOND TIME TRACK RECORD (+ = positive record. − = negative record)
Michael Bell	+	Ayr, Beverley, Hamilton, Newcastle, Newmarket (July), Redcar, Thirsk, Warwick, Windsor, York.
	−	Doncaster, Epsom, Folkestone, Kempton, Newmarket (Rowley), Nottingham.
Karl Burke	+	Beverley, Hamilton, Haydock, Ripon, Thirsk, Yarmouth.
	−	Doncaster, Newcastle, Newmarket (July), Southwell, Wolverhampton, York.
Paul Cole	+	Catterick, Chepstow, Folkestone, Leicester, Newbury, York.
	−	Chester, Doncaster, Goodwood, Haydock, Kempton, Newmarket (Rowley), Salisbury, Windsor, Wolverhampton.

Richard Fahey	+	Catterick, Haydock, Newcastle, Redcar, York.
	−	Ayr, Beverley, Ripon, Southwell, Thirsk.
Michael Jarvis	+	Doncaster, Goodwood, Haydock, Kempton, Lingfield (A/W), Newbury, Newmarket (July), Pontefract, Windsor, Yarmouth, York.
	−	Folkestone, Leicester, Newmarket (Rowley), Nottingham, Warwick, Wolverhampton.
Jeremy Noseda	+	Lingfield (A/W), Yarmouth, York.
	−	Newmarket (Rowley), Newmarket (July), Windsor.
Kevin Ryan	+	Ayr, Hamilton, Haydock, Leicester, Ripon, Southwell, Wolverhampton.
	−	Beverley, Carlisle, Catterick, Chester, Doncaster, Musselburgh, Newcastle, Nottingham, Redcar, Thirsk, Warwick, York.
Saeed Bin Suroor	+	Doncaster, Kempton, Leicester, Newbury, Newmarket (Rowley), Nottingham.
	−	Folkestone, Lingfield (A/W), Newmarket (July), Yarmouth.
Bryan Smart	+	Ayr, Beverley, Hamilton, Musselburgh, Newcastle, Pontefract, Redcar.
	−	Catterick, Haydock, Leicester, Nottingham, Thirsk, Wolverhampton.

Trainers in and out of form

Backing or laying horses would be considerably easier if every racing yard stayed at its peak of performance throughout the whole season. Unfortunately for the punter, some stables take time to hit top form with their horses or they suffer quiet periods when winners are few and far between. This can occur for a number of reasons.

Some yards are slow to start because of local, colder weather which affects how quickly horses 'come to hand' in terms of peak fitness and 'come into their coats' (lose their winter covering of thicker hair). Other yards may benefit from a kinder weather in the spring, their horses are more 'forward' and they are ready for an early start. For the punter, an inspection of the animals in the paddock or the pre-parade ring is often the only way to find out – unless the racing is covered on Channel Four. Thankfully, Channel Four's experts (John Francome and Jim McGrath) provide an outstanding service in this regard but the satellite channels rarely have the time for a paddock review. A gleaming 'coat' is a great sign whilst a dull or wintery coat means the animal may need more time.

Some yards get laid low by viruses which affect the well-being of their horses, whilst parasites such as ring worm can also impede performance. Obviously, at some stage, even the most laid-low of training establishments will break out of its winner-less doldrums but until that happens the odds are against winners appearing. For this reason, not many trainers like to admit that they have a problem – after all, owners might move their horses. Although it is not the norm, Jeremy Noseda was brave enough to announce such a problem with his horses at Royal Ascot in 2008 and he scrubbed several runners from the meeting after stable setbacks.

Thankfully, the information needed to find out which yard's hot and which is not, is available each day in *The Racing Post*. Their 'Post Data' column lists beside each day's race card, those trainers who are in or out of form. Their charts show a tick ($\sqrt{}$) to signify that a specific trainer has had at least one winner within the last 14 days, whilst a cross (X) signifies a fortnight of losers.

What implications does this have for the punter? First of all, it is sensible to avoid the yards that are out of form. Analysis of over 700 two year old runners, whose trainers were out of form, showed that over 90 per cent got beaten. However, there are potential opportunities for the brave punter to back the 'cold' trainers. They must come out of their cold phase sooner or later.

POINTERS

Check whether the trainer is out of form, or may be coming back to form.

The pace of progress

Since some yards are slower to come to hand than others, either because of the weather or because they focus on winning the more valuable end of season races, there is sense in knowing the typical pattern in the leading yards. Richard Hannon, for example, rarely has two year old runners in March but he soon hits his stride in April. Over the past five seasons, a quarter of his juvenile runners have won during that month. His two year olds also perform well in May and June, winning 20 per cent of their races but this starts to slip away by July.

By contrast, Mark Johnston's two year olds tend to take a little longer to get into their stride, possibly because of his North Yorkshire base. He still manages a very respectable winner to runner ratio of 17 per cent in May. However, his juveniles tend to perform best in July and August before tailing off slightly in October.

Channon, like Hannon, tends to start the season with a flourish, unless it's been a very cold winter in Berkshire. He can get winners in March but his best winner to runner ratio of 22 per cent tends to be in May. By September and October only 10 per cent of his two year old runners are winning.

It's difficult to take a hard and fast view regarding Bryan Smart, for each turf season he has improved his score of late. But on past performance, April is his best month for two year olds with a 29 per cent strike rate. By August and September his winner to runner ratio tends to deteriorate.

Kevin Ryan has few runners in March but soon starts popping in the winners in April and May with an average strike rate of 17 per cent. June is his best month with a 35 per cent strike rate over the past 5 years.

John Gosden has few two year old runners in April and May but likes to have one or two ready by late May or early June for Royal Ascot. His strike rate reaches

21 per cent by July and peaks at 26 per cent in August before dropping back slightly.

The move from Lambourn to Manton has changed Brian Meehan's strategy with his two year olds. Historically, he used to start early but nowadays April runners are rare and the yard tends to hit peak form with its two year olds from June onwards. Perhaps this is because Manton is high up on the Wiltshire Downs and horses tend to keep their winter coats for longer than in more sheltered Lambourn.

Like Meehan, Michael Jarvis tends to start gently and focus his fire power on the valuable autumn two year old races. He's extremely unlikely to have two year old runners in April or May but by September his juveniles are at their peak with a 25 per cent strike rate.

Unlike some of his southern competitors, Richard Fahey's Yorkshire base gets going early and his two year olds in March and April have an excellent strike rate. His winner to runner ratio dips slightly in summer before falling off further in the autumn.

Paul Cole is another who likes to get started early and has an excellent strike rate in the spring with May a particularly strong month to watch out for. Throughout the year, his performance remains pretty consistent but the ratio is significantly lower than in the spring and early summer. Table 15 summarises for the leading trainers the pattern of their strike rate over the months of the season.

Table 15: Trainer strike rate by calendar month (past 5 years)

TRAINER	March %	April %	May %	June %	July %	Aug %	Sept %	Oct %
Richard Hannon	0	25	20	20	13	10	11	8
Mark Johnston	---	14	17	12	24	20	18	13
Mick Channon	18	12	22	13	12	13	10	10
Bryan Smart	---	18	29	19	15	4	9	15
Kevin Ryan	17	16	17	35	14	14	11	10
John Gosden	0	50	15	19	21	26	21	18
Barry Hills	0	19	20	18	9	19	14	10
Brian Meehan	0	7	13	15	13	14	14	11
Michael Jarvis	---	---	11	14	10	16	25	15
Richard Fahey	50	25	13	11	13	10	10	7
Paul Cole	20	12	21	11	14	12	12	11
Sir Michael Stoute	---	---	0	13	19	17	20	23
Jeremy Noseda	---	50	32	26	31	15	12	22
Saeed Bin Suroor	---	---	36	24	32	18	28	24
Karl Burke	20	10	14	18	17	15	8	6
Michael Bell	100	19	19	15	14	12	11	11
William Haggas	---	50	0	22	18	11	12	13
David Evans	14	10	10	6	7	5	4	7
Ralph Beckett	50	13	6	21	16	15	14	9

Table 15 shows that Sir Michael Stoute doesn't really get going with his juveniles until July nowadays, and he tends to hit peak form in September and October. It is important for punters to watch out for any early juveniles of his that head for Royal Ascot. They may be rare but they have an excellent strike rate.

Jeremy Noseda seems to have two parts to his season. He does particularly well during late spring and summer, targeting the top meetings with his more precocious juveniles. Then, in August and September his strike rate declines before a strong finish in October.

The same cannot be said of Saeed Bin Suroor who seems to have changed his strategy with two year olds in recent seasons. Nowadays he runs very few juveniles before July and focuses his attention on getting winners in September and October. In the last three seasons, almost all his two year old winners have come in the autumn months. The chart shows a strong performance in May but that reflects his strategy from a few years ago.

Karl Burke has also adapted his strategy in recent years. The overall figures suggest that March is his best month for winners but nowadays he tends to have few runners in early spring, with his best strike rate occurring over the summer months.

Michael Bell's Newmarket yard tends to be ready early and has an excellent strike rate in April and May. March, on paper, looks outstanding with a 100 per cent record but this is from only one runner and winner in the past five years. His is a stable to follow when his two year olds hit top form.

Bell's near neighbour, William Haggas takes a different approach to two year old training with the bulk of his juveniles arriving on the racecourse from August onwards. However, the few he sends out in June and July have an excellent strike rate.

David Evans' Welsh yard tends to start the season early and most years he has his best strike rate in March before the bigger yards get going although his runners in April and May should also be respected.

Ralph Beckett's Whitsbury stable can also have its juveniles ready to win early and his 50 per cent strike rate in March is very compelling. However, he sends out a lot more two year old runners in the summer and his winner to runner ratio is particularly consistent in June.

POINTERS

Check a trainer's strike-rate pattern across the months – each one is slightly different.

Backing favourites

So far, we've looked in detail at debutants and second time out juveniles. But there's also money to be made from backing or laying two year olds that are a bit more 'exposed' – that is, those horses that have already had several runs. Some training yards do much better with their fancied horses than others.

Richard Hannon is an example of a trainer with a good record of his favourites winning. He runs around 130 two year olds each season, so the yard has a very good line to each individual's ability. Over the past eight years, punters who backed his two year old market leaders blindly (in non-handicaps) would have won 4 out of 10 races, netting £30 profit from a £1 stake.

Horses trained by Gosden, Meehan and Smart that go to the races with favourite status win on more than 40 per cent of occasions. Two other yards, Noseda's and Haggas's, achieve an even higher strike rate of nearly 50 per cent with their juvenile market leaders. Of course, the betting ring takes no chances with their runners and prices them accordingly, so favourite backers would have only made a small profit from each.

Somewhat surprisingly, Mick Channon, Barry Hills and Sir Michael Stoute have a poorer record with their market leaders and for the punter, this means there is some value in opposing them on the exchanges. Table 16 illustrates this and shows the strike rate alongside the money that was potentially to be lost or made by backing them.

Table 16: Success rate of two year old favourites - 2000 – 2008 (in non-handicaps)

TRAINER	% STRIKE RATE	PROFIT OR LOSS
Richard Hannon	41	+£30
Mark Johnston	45	-£10
Mick Channon	38	-£42
Bryan Smart	44	+£9
Kevin Ryan	34	-£15
John Gosden	47	+£21
Barry Hills	36	-£45
Brian Meehan	46	+£21
Michael Jarvis	43	+£1
Richard Fahey	27	-£22
Paul Cole	43	+£1
Sir Michael Stoute	39	-£44
Jeremy Noseda	48	+£1
Saeed Bin Suroor	41	-£17
Karl Burke	30	-£17
Michael Bell	38	-£21
William Haggas	48	+£6
David Evans	24	-£20
Ralph Beckett	32	-£12

Perhaps the best place to take on these favourites is at the tracks where our top trainers have the poorest record. Looking at results for the past nine years, you'd lose most money backing Richard Hannon's two year olds at Ascot (a loss of £58) and Kempton (-£57). Mark Johnston's least rewarding racecourses are Haydock (-£35) and Yarmouth (-£38). Opposing Mick Channon's juvenile runners at Salisbury (-£41) and Bath (-£36) is rewarding. Whilst Bryan Smart's will tend to lose most money at Wolverhampton (-£37) and Thirsk (-£33).

POINTERS

Know the courses where trainers perform least well.

Further down the list, Kevin Ryan makes his biggest losses at Wolverhampton (-£42) and John Gosden seems safest to oppose at Lingfield on the all weather (-£22). Barry Hills' juveniles lose most money on Newmarket's July Course (-£39) and at Doncaster (-£36). Whilst Brian Meehan's two year olds offer poor returns at Windsor (-£44) and Newmarket (July) (-£47). Michael Jarvis's juveniles are also unprofitable to follow on the July Course (-£33) whilst Richard Fahey's lose most money at York (-£39). The only other significant statistic to note is Karl Burke's two year old performance at Wolverhampton (-£37).

Of course, if your interest is in trying to oppose favourites, then perhaps the best place to take them on is at the tracks where our top trainers have the poorest record.

The 'seven day rule'

There's another important point of interest if you're backing or laying two year olds. I call it the seven day rule. Certain yards have a habit of racing juveniles within a week of their last racecourse appearance. Perhaps, they feel they can snatch some more prize money while the horse is in top form or maybe they want to punish the animal for an indifferent effort.

Either way, another race within seven days is bad news. I analysed the results of nearly 400 two year olds that were re-visiting the racecourse within seven days of an earlier outing. Around nine in ten were beaten, some at very short odds indeed. Those that did succeed were mostly winners of claimers and sellers where the opposition was possibly so poor that they were the only ones capable of scoring. Suffice to say, it's a lot safer to avoid these 'early returners' unless, of course, you want to lay them.

POINTERS

Juveniles that have had a run within the past seven days seldom win.

CHAPTER 4

Courses

COURSES

In this chapter, we explore the relationships between the racetrack, its size, location and topography and the degree to which particular two year olds are suited or disadvantaged. For the punter, variables relating to the track, along with all the other considerations, are important to note. There are courses that suit particular horses and it is worth knowing which are which.

The racetrack

One of the enduring delights of British horseracing is the stage on which the sport is played. Our racecourses offer greater visual variety than any other racing nation, and each has its distinct characteristics and differing ground conditions.

These differences impact on a racehorse's ability to win. Not least because horses come in all shapes and sizes, and some are better suited to particular tracks. For example, some tracks suit horses with stamina, others favour horses with speed. The main influences are topography and the quality of the ground. It is also asking a lot of a two year old to expect him to cope with the hurly burly and razmataz of the big meetings at Royal Ascot, York's Ebor Festival or Glorious Goodwood. So, there is no doubt that, owing to a number of factors in combination, some tracks are tricker to race at than others. This can affect inexperienced horses in particular and it means that there are laying opportunities for the punter 'in the know'.

Topography

Let us first consider the importance of topography. Courses tend to differ in four significant respects. Some place a strong emphasis on speed since they are flat or downhill in nature (e.g. Goodwood). Others place a greater emphasis on stamina since they have stiff, uphill finishes (e.g. Sandown). Racecourses are also described as flat or undulating. This differentiation is important since undulating surfaces, such as are found at Catterick or Folkestone, are not ideal for animals with a long-stride: they can become unbalanced.

Some tracks by contrast are described as 'sharp' in character. This means that they have tight bends and they suit neat, speedy types rather than resolute gallopers. Sharp tracks include Warwick, Ripon and Chester.

Knowing these differences and the course characteristics that are likely to suit a specific two year old are important factors when backing or laying them. For example, not many winners of the Lily Agnes Stakes at Chester go on to win the two year old sprint races over Royal Ascot's stiff straight, although quite a few try. Table 17 sets out the details of all the UK's turf tracks along with an interpretation about their suitability for particular styles of running.

POINTERS

Know your tracks and which tracks suit which horses.

Table 17: UK racecourses (turf), their topgraphical characteristics and suitedness to particular styles of racing

Ascot	Stiff, galloping, easy turns, no significant undulations, testing on soft.
Ayr	Relatively flat, gentle undulations, easy turns, galloping.
Bath	Relatively stiff and galloping, uphill from the turn.
Beverley	Very stiff sprint track that is testing for two year olds when soft.
Brighton	Sharp track with pronounced gradients and an emphasis on speed and experience, especially amongst two year olds.
Carlisle	Stiff, galloping and a significant stamina test for two year olds.
Catterick	Undulating with sharp turns and a falling gradient in the straight.
Chepstow	Relatively stiff, climbing over the final 5 furlongs, suits sharp two year olds.
Chester	Flat, sharp track on the turn most of the way. Won't suit long-striding gallopers.
Doncaster	Flat, galloping, easy turns.

Epsom	Races up to 8 furlongs are very sharp and mostly downhill not suiting long-striding gallopers or very inexperienced two year olds.
Folkestone	Undulating, easy turns and sharp in nature.
Goodwood	Sharp, with a steep downhill gradient, suiting speedsters with a fluent action.
Hamilton	Undulating, easy turns with a stiff run to the finish.
Haydock	Flat, galloping track with sharp turns.
Leicester	Stiff, galloping, easy turns. The sprint course can prove quite a test for two year olds on soft.
Lingfield	Sharp, downhill sprint track putting a premium on speed.
Musselburgh	Flat, slight undulations and sharp turns.
Newbury	Flat, slight undulations, galloping.
Newcastle	Stiff, particularly for two year olds, galloping with easy turns.
Newmarket (Rowley)	Some slight undulations with a distinct downhill run to the Dip followed by an uphill finish, galloping and stamina required.
Newmarket (July)	Similar to the Rowley course.
Nottingham	Flat, galloping, easy turns.
Pontefract	Stiff, sharp bend into straight, a test for two year olds on soft.
Redcar	Flat, galloping.
Ripon	Flat, undulations, sharp.

Salisbury	Stiff, galloping, a test for two year olds on soft.
Sandown	Very stiff on both the sprint track and round course, galloping, easy turns.
Thirsk	Slight undulations, easy turns, sharp.
Warwick	Sharp track, relatively flat over less than 1 mile, suits speedsters.
Windsor	Flat, sharp, tight bends.
Yarmouth	Flat, galloping track.
York	Flat, galloping, easy turns.

Britain's all-weather surfaces also have their own distinct characteristics :

Great Leighs	Flat, galloping, left-handed track with easy bends based on a polytrack surface (similar to a fast surface on grass.)
Kempton	Moderately sharp, right-handed track with average bends based on a polytrack surface.
Lingfield	Sharp, undulating, left-handed track with tight bends based on a polytrack surface.
Southwell	Flat, galloping track with an easy, left-handed turn based on fibresand (similar to a softer surface on grass.)
Wolverhampton	Flat, sharp, left-handed track with tight bends based on a polytrack surface (since 2004).

Another important fact to note is that the form on one all-weather track doesn't necessarily translate to another, despite most courses now using polytrack as the surface to race on. This is illustrative of the point that the topographical characteristics must be considered alongside the other characteristics of the surface or the track. None of these factors should be considered in isolation when punting.

Experience of the horse

For two year old juveniles, some tracks represent a particular challenge owing to their inexperience. Conversely, some tracks suit those much better who know what they're doing. I have analysed several hundred two year old races at different tracks in recent years. There is a marked difference in the number of races won by experienced horses as against newcomers. Part of this difference is explained by the fact that some trainers resist running their debutants at the trickier tracks – another reason for believing that the more quirky the conditions, the less likely that a first time out two year old will cope.

On average, during the first half of the season, about 65 per cent of all two year old races are won by horses with experience (In June, it's about 75 per cent). At eleven courses, the percentage of races won by those with previous experience is significantly higher. Epsom and Brighton with their difficult downhill cambers are particularly challenging for debutants. Laying newcomers at these and the other tracks listed below can pay dividends. Table 18 shows the effect of experience at Ascot or Southwell, for example, where it appears that experience matters hugely. Over 90 per cent of winners at these tracks are horses with experience – a strong indication that debutants are best left alone or laid.

Table 18: Pattern of winners at two years old by track

TRACK	THE PERCENTAGE OF WINNERS THAT HAVE EXPERIENCE
Ascot	90%
Beverley	75
Brighton	94
Catterick	81
Chester	83
Epsom	95
Redcar	81
Sandown	81
Southwell	94
Thirsk	86
Wolverhampton	85

POINTERS

Get to know which are the tricky tracks for newcomers.

Favouritism

Backing every favourite blindly despite their excellent strike rate would still lose you money. Interestingly, favourites do better at some courses than others. A review of the past nine years shows that favourites (in non handicaps) do particularly well at Chester (50 per cent winners to runners), Warwick (48 per cent), Pontefract (46 per cent), Brighton (45 per cent) and Carlisle (45 per cent). Backing them blindly at these courses would have been profitable, but not especially so.

The same analysis shows that favourites perform worst at Newcastle (34 per cent), Newbury (35 per cent), Goodwood (35 per cent) and Ascot (35 per cent). Backing favourites blindly at these tracks would have been a losing strategy.

The draw

A very important characteristic of the track concerns the significance of the draw - the numbered berth from which the racehorse starts. Historically, horses drawn closest to the running rail tend to be favoured because the rail helps them to run in a straight line. In addition, the ground closest to the rail can be compacted by years of galloping, making it quicker underfoot than, say, the middle of the track or the outside.

Two year olds are particularly susceptible to draw bias since they lack the experience to overcome any disadvantage. By contrast, older horses tend to have more understanding of what's required of them and their jockeys can find the animals more responsive to their requests to steer one way or another.

An outside draw represents a particular concern for owners of debutant two year olds. This stall, furthest away from the running rail (except when the stalls are placed in the centre of the course) provides a particular challenge for newcomers. Not only is the juvenile at the racetrack for the first time, he's in very close proximity to other horses on one side, the stalls are relatively unfamiliar, and on the other side there is a wide open space.

All too often, the crash of the stalls opening and the rapid exit of the other horses causes the debutants to spook. The animal's natural reaction is to shy away from the commotion which, in turn, loses it valuable lengths at the start. Some two year olds are smart enough to overcome this disadvantage but the large majority fail. In fact, in some 200 races that I've analysed, the juvenile debutant drawn furthest from the running rail lost on more than 95 per cent of occasions. Some were favourites and would have represented an excellent opportunity to lay a two year old on the exchanges.

POINTERS

Avoid debutants drawn furthest from the running rail.

Independent of the age of the horse, some tracks show a marked bias towards low or high numbered stalls. In other words, the winning chances of the horse are significantly affected by the draw – regardless of whether the draw places the horse near the rail. Furthermore, the bias can become more or less significant, and it can change in extremes of going. Table 19 lists the main UK tracks and shows whether there is a draw bias and, if so, under what conditions.

A relatively recent rule change by the racing authorities has further influenced the impact of the draw at some tracks. Since the late 90s, jockeys have been required to ride in a straight line from their draw position until reaching a marker pole. Only then may they move to the running rail (provided that interference does not result).

At courses like Chester or the all weather track at Lingfield over sprint distances, a railside draw is a major problem if the horse starts slowly. On sharp tracks like these, the bend may come too quickly for the horse to regain a position, and/or the race is over before recovery is possible.

Of course, some racecourses try to negate any draw bias by placing the stalls in the middle of the course. However, at Ascot, despite this, the draw bias seems to fluctuate between meetings. This is particularly noticeable at the Royal Ascot meeting when, in one year the low numbers are favoured, and in another they are not. I can only assume that either the rain missed part of the course, or that the watering system soaked one side of the track more than the other.

Whilst on the subject of Royal Ascot, here's another draw statistic to interest forecast backers. The winner and second placed horses in the Queen Mary have both been drawn next to each other six out of ten recent times. I'm not sure if this is just pure chance or whether it can be explained by watering. Either way, it is a statistic that is worth a small dual forecast because if you think you know the winner, then you should be confident that you can predict which horse is coming second!

POINTERS

Take careful note of the draw at the track in relation to the ground.

Table 19: The significance of the draw

TRACK	DRAW BIAS
Ascot	No significant advantage but a rails draw used to be helpful, especially on soft.
Ayr	High numbers in small fields over the straight course, but low in large fields.
Bath	Low numbers favoured, provided they can break fast.
Beverley	High numbers strongly favoured, except on soft when low numbers do better.
Brighton	Low numbers best.
Carlisle	High numbers best on fast, low slightly favoured on soft.

Catterick	Low numbers best but they need to break fast.
Chepstow	High numbers slightly favoured.
Chester	Low numbers strongly favoured provided they can break fast.
Doncaster	High numbers favoured, avoid a low draw in big fields.
Epsom	High numbers best over 5 furlongs but low over 6 furlongs and 7 furlongs.
Folkestone	High numbers best over 6 furlongs or in large 5 furlong fields. Otherwise low over 5 furlongs.
Goodwood	Low numbers best in sprints but stall one a disadvantage on the straight course. High numbers have a distinct advantage over 7 furlongs.
Great Leighs	No obvious advantage to date.
Hamilton	High numbers best on soft, low on fast ground. High numbers also have an advantage over 1 mile.
Haydock	High numbers favoured on soft.
Kempton	High numbers favoured in sprints, and especially at 5 furlongs.
Leicester	High numbers slightly favoured.
Lingfield (Turf)	High numbers best on fast, especially after recent rain.
Lingfield (A/W)	Low over 5 furlongs but stall one a disadvantage. 6 furlongs low numbers..
Musselburgh	Low numbers slightly favoured over 5 furlongs, high slightly favoured over further.

Newbury	High numbers favoured, especially on soft, but in very big fields low numbers can win from the far rail.
Newcastle	High numbers favoured on fast, low numbers on soft.
Newmarket (Rowley)	Slight advantage to those drawn nearest to running rail.
Newmarket (July)	Nearest to the running rail is best.
Nottingham	High numbers seem favoured on fast, low do better on soft.
Pontefract	Low numbers favoured in sprints, except on soft.
Redcar	Middle to high numbers best on straight course.
Ripon	Low numbers favoured on fast, high on soft, except in large fields when a rails draw helps.
Salisbury	High numbers favoured on fast, low on soft.
Sandown	High numbers best over 5 furlongs, especially on soft. Stall one is a big disadvantage in larger fields over 5 furlongs.
Southwell (A/W)	Centre best over 5 furlongs, low numbers best over 6 furlongs.
Thirsk	High numbers best in sprints, except on soft. Rail best if just watered.
Warwick	Low numbers favoured on fast, high numbers do better on soft.
Windsor	High numbers best in sprints, except on soft when low favoured.

Wolverhampton	Low numbers best over 5 furlongs and 6 furlongs.
Yarmouth	High numbers best in sprints, especially in larger fields.
York	Middle to high best on fast, low numbers slightly favoured on soft.

Variations in going

It is almost a truism to say that the going can make a big difference to a horse's chances of winning. A few years ago, I was the part owner of a colt called *Amaretto Bay*. He was a promising two year old who, like his sire *Common Grounds*, had a preference for good or softer going.

We entered him to run in the listed National Stakes at Sandown but his chances of victory were less than good owing to the fact that the ground was forecast to be fast. Thankfully for us, the heavens opened about an hour before his race, and the going changed from fast to the soft side of good. He relished the conditions and romped home at 10/1.

I use this as an illustration of how important it is to know the true state of the going before having a bet. Good ground in the morning can turn to bottomless going by the afternoon, if there's a downpour in the spring and autumn. By contrast, soft going in the summer months can dry out fast under a hot morning sun leaving it officially 'good' by the afternoon.

Some two year olds seem to cope on very heavy ground but get stuck on soft or good to soft because it's sticky and holding. This stickiness seems at its worst when a track has had a day or so to dry out from a deluge. I'm not a particular fan of running inexperienced two year olds on heavy or hard ground since it can take a long time to get over what is a very testing or jarring experience. For this reason, I'm wary of backing juveniles, early in the season if they have previously had a hard race on bottomless ground at one of the stiffer tracks such as Newcastle or Sandown.

I feel the same way about backing a two year old that has had a recent win on very hard ground. Although it is a rarity nowadays due to the existence of watering systems, there is still the occasional very hard surface. The risk is that it takes a significant toll on the young limbs of a two year old, leaving it unwilling to exert itself fully on a fast surface in subsequent races. Bath provides one such example. During the dry months, even though there is a good covering of turf, the course at Bath cannot be watered owing to its position on the top of the Downs.

It is difficult for the tracks to report accurately on the going since they have to provide an approximation for the whole of the course, rather than just a part of it. In the old days, racecourses tended to be less faithful to the truth and described the ground in terms more likely to encourage a good turnout of runners. However, the level of criticism from trainers and other interested parties, along with the arrival of new technology has changed things for the better.

From 2009, punters will, at last, get an official going 'reading' based on the findings of a hand-held, measuring device called a GoingStick. The new GoingStick measures the 'penetration' of the racing surface, in much the same way as a horse's hoof, so it should give a uniform guide to ground conditions that form students can use. However, the machine is apparently not failsafe. Readings are affected by soil type and equivalent readings are commonly interpreted in different ways at different tracks.

The reported state of the ground and, particularly any change in the going during the day of a race, provides an excellent opportunity for players on the betting exchanges. This is because the market doesn't always factor in how the draw can influence the outcome.

POINTERS

Be wary of two year olds that have won on extremes of going.

The class of race

Race classification is important to understand. Animals with more ability tend to compete in higher class races, whilst those with moderate ability stay in lower class contests. The better class races also offer higher prize money and prestige whilst the lower ones might make winning more certain.

Racecourses are graded into four different classes, based on the quality of their racing and the prize money available. Set out below in Table 20 is an abridged version of the full flat race classification scheme along with the prize money they currently offer. Table 21 lists the tracks by class of racing. Thankfully, the racing papers and online sites set this information out clearly and they also list the class of races that the horse has competed in previously.

Table 20: Races by class, type and prize money

CLASSES	RACE TYPES	APPROXIMATE PRIZE VALUES
Class 1	Group 1 Group 2 Group 3 Listed Races	£170,000 £ 80,000 £ 50,000 £ 30,000
Class 2	Conditions Stakes Nursery Handicaps (higher prize money)	£ 13,000+
Class 3	Conditions Stakes Novice Races Maidens (higher prize value)	£10,000 - £14,000
Class 4	Conditions Stakes Novice Races Maidens Nursery Handicaps Some Claimers and Sellers	£6,000 - £10,000
Class 5	Novice Races Nursery Handicaps Claiming and Selling races	£4,000 - £7,000
Class 6	Some Novice races Nursery Handicaps Claiming and Selling races	£3,000 - £5,000
Class 7	Classified Stakes	£3,000+

Table 21: Racetrack by class of racing

GRADE 1	GRADE 2	GRADE 3	GRADE 4
Ascot Epsom Goodwood Newbury Newmarket Sandown York	Ayr Chester Doncaster Haydock Kempton Newcastle Salisbury	Bath Beverley Chepstow Hamilton Leicester Lingfield (Turf) Nottingham Pontefract Redcar Ripon Thirsk Windsor Yarmouth	Brighton Carlisle Catterick Folkestone Lingfield (A/W) Musselburgh Southwell Warwick Wolverhampton

Note: Great Leighs has yet to be graded.

Horses that shift between classes will, in many instances, be facing a stiffer test or an easier opportunity. A horse I co-owned in 2008, called *Courageous Nature*, had some ability but not enough to win a maiden race. However, when we dropped him to selling class, he won well at the first opportunity and was snapped up by another trainer.

POINTERS

Look out for horses that are dropping down a class or going up.

At the beginning of the season, evidence that two year olds are being shifted from one class of race to another may not be all that significant. After all, there are only a few flat races each day from which to choose. By the summer there are many more, and this is the point from a betting point of view when it is worth noting when horses are being dropped in class to find a winning chance. Likewise, it is generally true that trainers who start their two year olds off in the better class races must think very well of them. Those that step up significantly in class having won a maiden must also be held in high regard at home.

That's not to say that owners don't occasionally ask their trainers to run their horses at the bigger meetings so they can have a fun day out. At Royal Ascot, there are always a smattering of two year olds entered at the owners' bidding because they'd like a good day out and want to have a runner. Of course, these animals have little or no hope of a win. Other owners who live abroad, or are race sponsors, like to see their horses run when they know that they'll be able to attend. Spotting these can be a bit of an art, but if you go racing, you should spend a short time scrutinising the owners in the paddock. A rarely seen tax-exile or a member of the Royal Family won't be wasting a journey to a minor meeting just for the trip.

We've already seen that some trainers will send horses to a variety of tracks and/or class of race in order to find a winning opportunity. But transporting racehorses around the country is a very expensive business so it does not go unnoticed by punters and layers when horses travel long distances.

From the owners' perspective, the cost of a return trip by horsebox from, say, Lambourn to Hamilton, some 370 miles in each direction, will be just under £1,000. Lambourn to Newcastle will be only slightly less at £750. Race entry costs and other expenses will add further to the expense. Furthermore, as some journeys are impossible in a day by road, the animal will have to be rested overnight at a strange location.

POINTERS

Look out for two year olds that are the trainer's only runner at a distant race meeting.

Most horseboxes will carry sufficient water and feed for the horse's return trip but some animals don't travel well and won't eat up, due to anxiety. They are therefore unsettled come race day and might also lack sufficient energy to perform at their best. Travelling therefore presents a variety of different problems.

From a punter's perspective, backing horses that have travelled long distances can pay dividends, especially if the trainer has only the one runner at the meeting. However, paddock inspection is important. A two year old that is sweating or 'on its toes' (agitated) in the parade ring might just have 'run its race' on the journey up.

Race times

Some sceptics might take the view that a half second here or there is really irrelevant in the hurly burly of a horse race run on an uneven grass surface. However, the scientists tell us that in a 5 furlong race, a horse will travel over 6 lengths in just one second. They also tell us that you would need to add or take off 22lbs from the weight the jockey has to carry in order to make a difference of a second over the same distance. Time therefore tells us a lot about ability.

POINTERS

Race times can be used to differentiate between moderate animals and more promising ones.

Experts also tell us that the last furlong of a five furlong race is run more slowly than the others, the winner getting home just better than the rest. This means that a two year old winner putting up a faster than average time over five or six furlongs on good ground, carrying around 9 stone, is almost certainly a smart individual.

Racing professionals and organisations such as Timeform make a living from assessing time performances accurately. I personally pay particular attention to the speed rating in *The Racing Post* but I also like to see Timeform's two year old ratings, since the authors have many years experience in judging the merit of individual performances.

The speed rating experts, such as Timeform, take the track, weight and ground conditions into consideration when calculating their performance figures, but it's quite expensive to buy this information on a daily basis.

In general, the shorter the race, the more 'flat out' speed is required to win. This means that a fast performance from a two year old, that predominantly races over sprint distances, is very good indicator of exceptional ability.

It can be difficult to assess the difference between a good winning time and a moderate one. I find it more helpful to spot what might be an above average performance than to try to differentiate moderate juveniles on the basis of small differences in track times. I have therefore drawn up a list, by racecourse, of what constitutes a better than average time performance by a two year old. Table 22 shows what constitutes a fast time for a two year old over five furlongs and it should help the punter wanting to make a judgement about a good or a poor time for a particular winning performance by an individual runner.

It is important to note that this analysis tends to be more useful for highlighting promising performances at the lower grade tracks than at the likes of Ascot. This is because, at Ascot, almost all two year old winners need to be above average in ability and/or experience. Conversely, a very slow time at Ascot might raise questions about the quality of the form.

Table 22: Performances of merit (judged by time) over 5 furlongs

TRACK	GOOD OR FASTER	SOFT
Ascot	Under 62 seconds	Under 65 seconds
Ayr	Under 60 seconds	?
Bath	Under 62 seconds	Under 64 seconds
Beverley	Under 63 seconds	Under 66 seconds
Brighton	Under 62 seconds	?
Carlisle	Under 61 seconds	Under 64 seconds
Catterick	Under 60 seconds	Under 62 seconds
Chepstow	Under 60 seconds	?
Chester	Under 61 seconds	Under 63 seconds
Doncaster	Under 60 seconds	Under 61 seconds
Epsom	?	?
Folkestone	Under 60 seconds	---
Goodwood	Under 60 seconds	Under 63 seconds
Great Leighs	?	?
Hamilton	Under 60 seconds	Under 64 seconds
Haydock	Under 62 seconds	Under 63 seconds
Kempton	?	n/a
Leicester	Under 61 seconds	Under 64 seconds
Lingfield (Turf)	Under 58 seconds	?
Lingfield (A/W)	Under 60 seconds	n/a
Musselburgh	Under 60 seconds	?
Newbury	Under 61 seconds	Under 62 seconds

Newcastle	Under 61 seconds	?
Newmarket (Rowley)	Under 61 seconds	Under 63 seconds
Newmarket (July)	?	?
Nottingham	Under 61 seconds	Under 63 seconds
Pontefract	Under 64 seconds	Under 66 seconds
Redcar	Under 59 seconds	?
Ripon	Under 60 seconds	Under 61 seconds
Salisbury	Under 61 seconds	Under 63 seconds
Sandown	Under 62 seconds	Under 63 seconds
Southwell (A/W)	Under 60 seconds	---
Thirsk	Under 60 seconds	Under 63 seconds
Warwick	Under 60 seconds	Under 63 seconds
Windsor	Under 60 seconds	Under 62 seconds
Wolverhampton	Under 62 seconds	---
Yarmouth	Under 62 seconds	Under 63 seconds
York	Under 60 seconds	Under 61 seconds

? = insufficient evidence

Table 23 lists the top five speediest and least speedy racecourses over five and six furlongs. The fastest five furlong course in Britain is at Epsom where the course record for two year olds stands at 55 seconds and the slowest is Wolverhampton. Over six furlongs, the fastest is Epsom again, whilst Pontefract and Southwell (the all weather track) are the slowest.

Table 23: Fastest and slowest 5 and 6 furlong tracks

COURSE RECORDS (Two Year Olds)		5 FURLONGS	seconds	6 FURLONGS	seconds
Fastest	1	Epsom	55.02	Epsom	67.85
	2	Redcar	56.90	Brighton	68.10
	3	Ayr	56.98	Lingfield (Turf)	68.60
	4	Lingfield (Turf)	57.18	Bath	68.70
	5	Thirsk	57.20	Redcar	68.84
Slowest	5	Carlisle	60.10	Ascot	72.46
	4	Yarmouth	60.40	Wolverhampton	72.61
	3	Beverley	61.00	Chester	72.85
	2	Pontefract	61.10	Southwell (A/W)	74.00
	1	Wolverhampton	61.13	Pontefract	74.00

POINTERS

The winner almost invariably has an easier race than the horse that is second.

For the individual runner, race times are, of course, greatly affected by going and the weight carried. For example, I used to own a moderate two year old called *Knight Onthe Tiles* who managed to break the six furlong course record at Warwick in a nursery – he completed the race in 71 seconds. What made this achievement possible, however, was the combination of very firm ground and the low weight he was set to carry. It didn't follow that he was able to reproduce the performance elsewhere. In fact, all he subsequently managed to win was a claimer – a fact which pretty much sums up the extent of his ability. It is also worth remembering that in most races, the second horse has a harder race than the winner (unless, of course, he's unlucky in running). He has, in all probability, ran his hardest to reach second place. The winner might still have something in-hand.

Chapter 5

Jockeyship

JOCKEYSHIP

It is very important for the punter to understand what one might call 'the jockey factor' in relation to horses to be backed or laid. It is a very brave jockey indeed that rides an unraced or very lightly raced two year old and the task of riding an inexperienced juvenile is not a challenge for the faint-hearted. As the performance of jockeys varies in some systematic ways, this chapter sets out the patterns it is important to understand.

Bravery

A jockey needs to be brave to ride a two year old well because a relatively inexperienced juvenile is still learning and can be unpredictable. Owners who have seen twenty skittish debutant two year olds being led round the paddock will not need reminding of this. It is not uncommon, for example, for a juvenile to rear up, or gallop off in the direction of the stables, scattering connections in blind panic. It is also not unusual for the jockey arriving on the scene a moment later to be told that the animal is as good as gold at home – and remember that most of them will never have ridden the horse before.

Getting to the start can be a bit traumatic for the horse as well as the rider. I used to own a speedy two year old called *Masterstroke*, who was fine going into the stalls but didn't like staying there. On one occasion at Windsor, with Pat Eddery in the saddle, he managed to escape from under the starting gate, scraping Pat off in the process. *Masterstroke* then galloped back to the stables with his saddle wrapped round his nether regions, demolishing a metal gate in the process. Thankfully, neither horse nor jockey was injured. But pity the poor owner who may have travelled miles to see this happen.

Siena Gold was another who was no fan of the stalls and Frankie McDonald, who won the Super Sprint on her, told me that he'd practically 'made love to her' in the gate to keep her calm and relaxed.

Judgement

There are a number of factors over and above basic race-riding ability that the jockey needs to consider. First, is the degree to which the horse is considered to be 'a bit green'. What this describes is a horse's inability to understand what's required of him or her. This isn't the fault of the jockey or trainer but just a slowness on the horse's behalf to understand what it is supposed to do.

There's no easy way of spotting greenness in advance unless you are at the track and take time out for a paddock inspection. Skittish two year olds, the ones nervously prancing around the parade ring, and those whinnying for their mothers are certainly showing some immaturity in the preliminaries so there's every chance that they'll race 'green' as well. Good jockeyship can make all the difference.

For example, in 2008, I co-owned a two year old called *Wave Aside*. On his first ever outing at Windsor, he almost literally fell out of the stalls through greenness, giving the others a considerable head start. But by mid-way through the race, he'd worked out what he needed to do, thanks to some strong signals from Ted Duncan. He finished nearer first than last and next time out he had a much better idea of what was required of him. He demolished some decent opposition in a Newbury maiden without being given a hard race by Frankie Dettori. A neat illustration of what good jockeyship is all about on both counts.

A second factor to do with good jockeyship concerns the extent to which he or she gives the animal a punishing ride first time out. A seriously bad experience in this regard can sour the horse for ever more. Certainly as an owner, you don't want the whip used excessively or for the horse to be given an unnecessarily hard race that will leave a mark on the memory. Furthermore, the racing authorities accept that it's not in the best welfare interests of the animal to hit it very hard when its chance of winning has gone. However, it is also against the rules of racing to use the race as a schooling opportunity, or give the horse such a tender ride that there is no hope of winning at all.

Finding the right balance between these extremes is a skilled business; it requires judgement and some of the best and worst jockeys identify themselves in the degree to which they judge wisely how hard to push their mount.

Special skill with two year olds

It's hard to say if some jockeys have a better way with two year olds than others. But the 'stats' show that some have a much better success rate, helped no doubt by the fact that they ride for yards with large strings of talented juveniles. I looked at data relating to the top 20 or so riders based on their overall success in the jockeys championship of 2008. However, I also analysed their individual success rates with two year olds over the past nine years, since I think that performance over the long term is more meaningful.

Table 24: Jockeys : their success rate on two year olds 2000 – 2008 (non-handicaps)

Jockey	% Winners to rides	% Placed horses to rides	Profit or Loss (£1)
Richard Hughes	19	47	-£82
Ryan Moore	15	42	-£296
Jamie Spencer	19	46	-£201
Neil Callan	13	37	-£201
Paul Hanagan	11	33	-£68
Seb Sanders	14	36	-£288
Jimmy Fortune	17	43	-£235
Dane O'Neill	11	36	-£653
Tom Eaves	8	26	-£263
Darryll Holland	13	37	-£426

Jim Crowley	8	25	-£88
Ted Durcan	11	34	-£538
Philip Robinson	15	37	-£125
Eddie Ahern	11	33	-£454
George Baker	7	21	-£265
Joe Fanning	13	35	-£330
Chris Catlin	9	26	-£599
Frankie Dettori	25	54	-£74
Richard Hills	16	48	-£309
Alan Munro	13	34	-£85
Steve Drowne	12	32	-£361

As Table 24 shows, the clear leader is Frankie Dettori, both in terms of winners to runners and placed horses to runners. Over the past nine years, he's won a quarter of all his two year old non-handicap rides and has been placed on more than half. Godolphin, the stable for which Dettori usually rides, is obviously a big factor in his general success but as more than two thirds of the above rides came from other yards, Dettori's ability has far more to do with him than the horses he is given. Sadly, backing Frankie on every two year old in a non-handicap would have lost you £74 (to £1). However, it is also true that he loses significantly less money than almost all of the rest. If you backed him just on favourites you'd be marginally ahead, even though it's true that the bookies clearly have his measure.

One jockey missing from this list is Kieren Fallon, who has nearly as good a strike rate on two year olds as Frankie Dettori. So, if he does return to the saddle, his juvenile rides should be treated with the utmost respect. Amongst the other jockeys with outstanding strike rates on juveniles are Richard Hughes (19 per cent winners to runners), Jamie Spencer (19 per cent), Jimmy Fortune (17 per cent) and Richard Hills (16 per cent). Each of these extremely effective jockeys as far as two year olds are concerned also manages to get almost half of all their juvenile rides to finish in the frame (in non-handicaps). But backing them blindly isn't an option and there are several others on the list who would be much more profitable to oppose.

POINTERS

Look at who are the effective and the less effective jockeys riding two year olds.

Jockeys and the courses

It's long been known that some jockeys ride certain courses better than others and, since riding juveniles requires particular skills in the saddle, it makes sense to focus on the tracks at which each rider excels. It is particularly important if you decide you must back a debutant because we have already seen that this isn't easy.

A jockey's strike rate at a course will partly be due to qualities in the horse, and partly due to the extent to which this and attributes (e.g. topography) of the track play to the jockey's strengths and experience. For example, I remember when the great Steve Cauthen first rode in Britain in the 80s, he struggled to master the challenges of Ascot racecourse. Once he did master it he was as good a rider of the course as both Lester Piggott and, more recently, Frankie Dettori.

One pointer for the punter therefore concerns whether the jockey on board has a good strike rate at the course. Table 25 shows the percentage strike rate with two year olds for the leading jockeys and the track where the wins occurred. The relevant statistics for this are also shown on the racing pages of the papers and in the race card.

POINTERS

Make sure the jockey has a good strike **rate at the course, but go carefully if you plan to lay the jockeys with the least luck.**

Table 25: Course by course performance of the top jockeys: 2004 – 2008
(ten rides or more at the track)

RACECOURSE	Hughes %	Moore %	Spencer %	Callan %	Hanagan %	Sanders %	Fortune %
Ascot	9	7	13	6	*	0	17
Ayr	---	*	*	26	19	*	---
Bath	18	22	22	*	*	22	21
Beverley	---	*	*	22	14	*	*
Brighton	29	24	*	*	---	14	*
Carlisle	---	---	*	*	10	*	---
Catterick	---	*	*	17	11	12	---
Chepstow	42	*	*	*	---	*	*
Chester	*	*	9	14	0	15	*
Doncaster	13	17	27	9	11	14	4
Epsom	*	20	*	*	*	*	---
Folkestone	44	21	33	---	---	13	*
Goodwood	19	11	0	0	*	15	17
Hamilton	---	*	*	*	17	*	---
Haydock	25	*	*	12	18	10	*
Kempton	20	22	16	7	*	13	19
Leicester	27	10	20	13	*	17	8
Lingfield (Turf)	13	24	*	*	---	24	*
Lingfield (A/W)	21	18	23	24	31	8	9

Musselburgh	---	*	0	7	5	14	*
Newbury	18	5	4	5	*	3	11
Newcastle	*	---	*	11	19	40	---
Newmarket (Rowley)	17	13	17	3	*	10	17
Newmarket (July)	17	15	15	18	*	0	21
Nottingham	*	25	9	4	*	14	14
Pontefract	*	*	27	7	7	18	*
Redcar	*	*	21	15	9	24	---
Ripon	*	*	*	27	3	25	---
Salisbury	19	15	17	---	---	14	21
Sandown	17	20	6	*	*	15	21
Southwell (A/W)	*	*	40	23	8	36	*
Thirsk	---	---	30	18	8	*	---
Warwick	15	36	35	*	*	9	*
Windsor	20	19	17	*	---	9	10
Wolverhampton	25	18	34	16	13	25	12
Yarmouth	*	29	20	8	*	16	13
York	9	12	16	15	6	0	11

(* = less than 10 rides at the track between 2004 – 2008)

(--- = no rides at the track between 2004 – 2008)

What Table 25 shows is that whilst Richard Hughes seems to ride two year olds well at every track, he particularly excels on some of the more undulating courses such as Brighton, Chepstow and Folkestone.

Ryan Moore, by contrast, another great all-rounder, has an excellent strike rate on the sharper tracks where keeping a horse balanced is of the utmost importance. The slight exception to his performance is Newbury, where only five per cent of his two year old rides have won in the past five seasons.

Newbury also seems to be an unlucky course for Jamie Spencer, but not as unlucky as Goodwood seems to be. In the last five seasons, Jamie Spencer has had 20 juvenile rides at the course and not one has won. However, he does particularly well at some of the all-weather tracks and he can ride galloping tracks and tricky surfaces with equal aplomb.

Neil Callan has a good record on most of the northern tracks, as well as Lingfield on the all-weather but he does best on courses such as Ripon and Ayr. Like Jamie Spencer, he's been out of luck at Goodwood in recent seasons with 19 losing juvenile rides in succession.

Paul Hanagan does particularly well at Lingfield on the all-weather. It is therefore surprising that he's not had a recent two year old winner at Chester from 14 rides since the courses are equally tight; Ripon is also an unlucky course for him.

Ex-champion jockey, Seb Sanders, has a pretty good all-round strike rate but like his co-champion, Spencer, he hasn't done well on juveniles at Newbury over the years. His voodoo courses are Ascot (14 losing juvenile rides), York (12 losing) and the Newmarket July Course (28 losing).

Jimmy Fortune is another consistent rider of two year olds who does particularly well at courses such as Sandown, Newmarket and Salisbury where there are stiff uphill finishes.

Amongst the other jockeys, O'Neill does well at Chepstow but seems unlucky at Newbury, Doncaster and Newmarket. Tom Eaves has a great strike rate at Ayr, Musselburgh and York but has had 27 losing juvenile rides in succession at Doncaster.

Darryll Holland rides Sandown and Southwell extremely well and also has an above average strike rate on juveniles at Bath and Goodwood. Jim Crowley is another who rides the downhill courses well with above average results at Goodwood and Brighton. However, he hasn't ridden a juvenile winner at Salisbury or Warwick over the last five years.

In contrast, Ted Duncan hasn't ridden a single two year old winner at Bath or Goodwood in the past five years, the latter from 37 rides. But he does particularly well at Doncaster and Newbury.

All courses come alike to Philip Robinson who has an excellent juvenile strike rate wherever he performs, perhaps with the exception of Windsor. He does particularly well at Pontefract with a 46 per cent strike rate.

Eddie Ahern is a past master of riding juveniles at sharp courses such as Chester, Lingfield, Warwick and

Southwell. He's also pretty effective at galloping tracks such as Haydock. His unluckiest course is Ascot, with 18 uninterrupted losing rides on two year olds.

George Baker knows what it takes to win at Lingfield on the all-weather although he's not had much luck on juveniles at Sandown and Newbury.

Chris Catlin certainly knows how to ride trickier tracks and does particularly well at Chester and Goodwood. However, he hasn't hit the target at Newbury, the Newmarket July Course or Ascot with his juvenile rides in recent years.

Frankie Dettori, like Philip Robinson and Richard Hughes, seems to be equally adept at getting two year olds to win at all the major tracks. His best strike rates are at Nottingham, Lingfield (A/W) and Leicester. The same can be said for Richard Hills, with a couple of exceptions. His strike rate at Doncaster and Nottingham is slightly disappointing.

Alan Munro does particularly well on two year olds at difficult tracks such as Ascot and Sandown but has been unlucky over recent years at Warwick.

Steve Drowne has not had much good fortune at Goodwood with his juvenile rides in recent seasons, losing on all 30. However, he has an enviable strike rate at Southwell and Chepstow.

Apprentices

At the other end of the spectrum in terms of their experience and knowledge of the game, are apprentice riders. Some are well worth their 'claim' (the pounds that they are allowed to deduct from the horse's allotted weight) especially if they ride a two year old at home and have come to understand the animal well. However, for some apprentices, the lack of race riding experience counts against them since they lack the knowledge to take full advantage of the gaps and openings that appear as a race unfolds.

It is interesting to note that there aren't any two year old races that are exclusively confined to apprentice riders and I am sure that this is because the combined inexperience of both jockey and horse is unlikely to prove productive. Despite this, there are still some trainers who put a 7lb claiming jockey on a debutant juvenile. Although it doesn't happen very often, I have analysed over 100 examples in recent years. Not surprisingly, over 95 per cent of them were beaten.

'Novice' apprentices don't do a great deal better in other two year old contests, despite their 7lb claim being worth about two lengths in a sprint over five or six furlongs. My records show that they lose on 92 per cent of occasions.

POINTERS

It's better to avoid backing 7lb claimers, but you can lay them.

Stable jockeys

It is not uncommon to see longstanding partnerships between trainers and particular jockeys, and the status that Frankie Dettori has with the Godolphin yard is perhaps the best example. However, not all trainers have such an arrangement and some, like Brian Meehan, prefer to book the best available jockey on the day. Mark Johnston's strategy, according to the media, is to book jockeys who are showing the best recent form. This also appears to be a very sound idea since confidence in the saddle seems to communicate itself to the horse.

Backing jockey-trainer combinations, where they exist, can be an effective way of finding winners but it doesn't work with every yard. Looking at recent results by trainer and jockey, there are some trends that are worth pursuing. However, the relationship between rider and trainer isn't always plain sailing, so caution is required. I have summarised some of my findings below:

Richard Hannon uses a considerable number of jockeys for his juveniles but Richard Hughes has the best strike rate on his horses of 20 per cent winners to rides (over the past nine years). Despite this, however, you would not have made money backing them blindly.

Mark Johnston is another who uses a wide variety of jockeys but Greg Fairley and Royston French have the best record on his two year olds. And at Bryan Smart's, Richard Mullen has an impressive 46 per cent strike rate on the yard's juveniles and a profitable return. By contrast, there is no obvious jockey to follow in Mick Channon's yard.

Neil Callan gets the most juvenile rides at Kevin Ryan's but Fergal Lynch and Paul Mulrennan have a slightly better strike rate. John Gosden does well with Jimmy Fortune but Frankie Dettori has an even better strike rate from fewer rides and is also profitable to follow.

The juvenile winners at Barry Hills's yard tend to be ridden by his sons, Michael and Richard, but if you followed them blindly, they both would lose you money. But at Michael Jarvis's, the juveniles ridden by Philip Robinson and Neil Callan are worth a punt.

Brian Meehan has his best strike rate with Frankie Dettori but there's no money to be made backing the partnership per se.

Richard Fahey relies on Paul Hanagan to steer home most of his two year old winners but Paul Cole uses the best available on the day, so there are no obvious trends.

Ryan Moore, Sir Michael Stoute's stable jockey, rides most of the yard's two year olds to victory but, again, you would have lost money backing them all.

A better strategy is to back the Jeremy Noseda juveniles ridden by Shane Kelly and Frankie Dettori, both of whom are profitable to back blindly. In fact, Dettori has, over the years, had a slightly better strike rate on Noseda's two year olds than for his retained stable of Godolphin and Saeed Bin Suroor, but the difference is marginal.

There are no obvious trends from Karl Burke's yard or at David Evans's, but Michael Bell has a good strike rate with Jamie Spencer and an improving one with Hayley Turner. Liam Jones seems to be the jockey of choice at William Haggas's yard for juveniles. Finally, Seb Sanders seems to be the rider of choice at Ralph Beckett's yard when the juveniles have a winning chance and he is also profitable to follow.

Communication

One of the other important strengths that the best jockeys bring to race riding of two year olds, and in fact all their rides, is their ability to articulate what they have learnt about the horse as a result of taking the ride. Sadly for the punter, this information is often only available to connections but I, for one, am always particularly interested in a top jockey's verdict on a debutant two year old. It can add hugely to the quality of the owner's experience at the track, as well as adding to his or her knowledge about the horse – a good way to manage the owners' expectations, provided the communication is given skilfully.

There is, of course, also no doubt that effective information provided by the jockey adds a crucial dimension for the trainer when designing the training regime or planning future race entries. All the more important that the communication is accurate and that judgement is used in its delivery.

The top jockeys have two important advantages when it comes to clear communication. First, they ride a great many juveniles so they have an excellent yard-stick on which to base their opinions. Second, and as their careers don't depend on pleasing the owners of a poor performer they are more likely to be honest in their remarks. Lesser jockeys, perhaps partly because they are also on the lesser horses and possibly less aware than the experienced jockeys that this is the case, tend to want to please. Perhaps, they hope to get more rides from the yard if they speak to the connections in exclusively positive terms.

I remember a post-race summary from several years ago provided by a jockey who had just finished one from last on a debutant of mine, beaten a long way by the winner. He summed up his learning in the time-honoured six words: "he gave me a nice feel". We did eventually find out a bit more about the horse and he went on to win a few races, so maybe the jockey was right after all, but it made me wonder how positive the comments must have been about the horses that beat us.

In my experience, the experts at the post-race analysis are Richard Hughes, Jamie Spencer, Jimmy Fortune and Frankie Dettori. Frankie Dettori can also add considerable value with his post-race observations, delivered in a very succinct manner. He may enjoy playing to the crowd, but no-one should doubt for a second his sheer professionalism when debriefing connections. Jamie Spencer rode a debutant that I have a small share of called *Navajo Nation*. He was able to provide very helpful advice on the most suitable going and trip for the horse going forward, whilst also advising us that the animal would do better as a three year old – as the horse is in training this year, I'll know soon enough whether this is the case.

What the jockeys say

I asked several world class jockeys and retired jockeys to name the best two year olds they had ever ridden, and what were the qualities that made the horse so special. Their answers were also illuminating:

Lester Piggott (*J.O.Tobin*)

'Of all the good two year olds I rode, I thought *J.O.Tobin* was the most exciting. He was a very good looking horse and always worked superbly. He won his three races in the UK in a canter but was beaten in the Grand Criterium when he was very upset before the start. He raced in the USA afterwards where he showed how good he was.'

Pat Eddery (*Zafonic*)

'He was massive and so much more mature than any other two year old I have ever ridden. He didn't just win … he annihilated the opposition.'

Ray Cochrane (*Chief Singer*)

'He had a fabulous physique, blistering speed and was very imposing. He was electric.'

Bruce Raymond (*Bitty Girl*)

'She was an amazing filly with blistering speed but the secret to her success was Michael Jarvis's training regime. I can only remember her being galloped twice in her life. He kept her race fit using a lunging rein.'

Kevin Darley (*Celtic Swing*)

'Every now and then a natural athlete comes along like Celtic Swing. He was very laid back in his slower paces but once you asked him to go he was like a Ferrari.'

Jimmy Fortune (*Oasis Dream*)

'A real straightforward horse with a great temperament and blistering speed. A total pleasure to ride.'

Neil Callan (*Amadeus Wolf*)

'I first rode him at the Newmarket breeze-ups and was impressed but he went out unsold. Thankfully, Kevin Ryan bought him privately and the horse soon started to show his class. I rode him in his first piece of serious work in a racecourse gallop at Ripon and he beat the lead horse, a highly rated older sprinter, by ten lengths. This performance blew us away and we knew we had something special.'

Jamie Spencer (*Crowded Horse*)

'It was his turn of foot that most impressed me. I've never had another horse pick up like he did in the Racing Post Trophy.'

Chapter 6

Weight

WEIGHT

Weight is the great leveller in horse racing. The amount one horse has to carry in relation to another, in the form of a jockey, his saddle and weight cloth, is the means by which the sport brings animals of different ability into closer competition. In this chapter I outline the essential differences between the various forms of handicap and the implications for the punter.

When races are run at level weights and every horse is carrying the same load on its back, then it follows that the animal with best ability should always win. This is fine at the highest level of competition since it determines the true champion. However, if all races were run without any penalties for prior success, then only the best horses would ever win. The odds would be prohibitively short and most owners would never own a winner.

The rating

Over the course of the juvenile's racing year, the handicapper may award a 'rating' (a weight to carry) that reflects the exact ability of the horse. Handicap ratings climb from zero to above 100 for the very best. Although the handicapper is not obliged to give a horse a rating unless and until the horse is entered for a nursery, some horses are given a rating if they have run in a particularly notable race or raced against other runners that already have a rating. The higher the rating a horse is given then the better the handicapper thinks he is. A juvenile rated 80 is, in the handicapper's judgement 10lbs better in performance terms than a horse he rates at 70, so in a nursery it will be required to carry 10lbs more.

The handicapper's aim in rating the horse is to give each runner an equal chance of winning and, for him, the perfect result is a multiple dead-heat. When the weight carried by each horse varies according to the experts' estimates of his ability, there is not only the opportunity for the lesser horses to have a theoretically equal chance on the day, there's an opportunity for the punter to back his own judgement.

In order for the punter to have an edge over the bookies, it is absolutely essential to understand the differences between 'maiden' and 'median' auction races, the ins and outs of nurseries or the significance of penalties in novice and conditions races. Why? Because all these races involve some form of penalty in terms of weight, and weight obviously influences the horse's chance of winning. I have been amazed over the years by the number of owners and racing fans who don't understand this and what the system of weight penalties mean for backing or laying a runner.

The races

Maiden Races

Possibly the easiest type of race to understand, and perhaps the most common as far as juveniles are concerned is the maiden race – open to horses that have never won. There are maidens for fillies, and maidens open to both sexes. Every colt and gelding must carry the same weight, but fillies running against them carry 5lbs less, reflecting their generally lesser strength. A 5lb allowance is quite generous, and should not be ignored by the punter.

The majority of two year olds start their racing lives in maiden races of some form or another and then progress in one of two directions. If they are of medium or moderate ability, then their future lies in nurseries, claimers or sellers. If they show considerable promise, then they are more likely to compete in conditions races and Group contests.

Median Auction Races

Next up are median auction races. These are also pretty straightforward in that the same rules as in maiden races regarding weight apply, but there is a subtle difference. These races are only open to two year olds by sires whose progeny were relatively cheap to purchase at the yearling sales. Each race sets its own limit to entry based on the middle price of a stallion's yearlings – so in one race, the median price might be £35,000 guineas, and in another, the price will be different. This usually means that expensively bred two year olds are not eligible to run – a sort of handicapping by stallion values.

Maiden Auction Races

Entry to maiden auction races is also restricted to the cheaper horses but in a significantly different way. Again, each race sets its own conditions of entry. Horses have to have cost less than a certain price at auction. Typically, a lower grade maiden auction will be restricted to two year olds that cost less than, say, £15,000 or £35,000. However, the really important thing to note is that the weight each two year old is set to carry is determined by the price. This means that the cheapest horses in the race could be carrying as much as 9lbs less than the most expensive, an advantage equivalent to two and a half lengths.

Novice Races

Novice races are common in the early part of the season and provide prior two year old winners with an opportunity to pick up more prize money, since they are no longer eligible for maiden races. It is important to note that debutants and maidens are eligible to run in novice races. However, such horses are likely to be taking on competition with considerably more experience and previously demonstrated ability.

To level the playing field in novice races, previous winners are penalised by having to carry extra weight, based on the class of race (prize money) that they have previously won. However, the win has to have been in other than a seller or a claimer because these wins are exempt. The penalties can range from 2lbs to 14lbs.

Conditions Races & Listed Contests

Conditions races are very similar to novice races but they tend to carry more prize money. Listed contests offer yet more money and the penalties for previous winners only kick in if the horse has already won a high class race.

Group Races

Some of the Group races for two year olds carry penalties and some don't. The penalties are not particularly high but they do make it tougher for the animals that have to carry them.

Nurseries

Nurseries, which start in July, are handicaps for two year olds. They are characterised, amongst other things, by the fact that the runners are all given a rating, published not less than five days in advance. Horses are only eligible for nurseries after three runs but not before, unless they have had a win – in which case they are eligible to enter with only one or two runs to their name. In addition, if they haven't won before a date in early September (after which the rule ceases to apply) they also need to have finished in the first four.

As we will see later, this information is significant for the punter. For one thing, horses that have had a previous and very recent win in another nursery will also be given a penalty over and above the weight dictated by their rating. This will arise if the handicapper hasn't had time to amend the rating since that win – a reason why some trainers like to run a horse in another nursery quickly – there is always the chance that the penalty will be lower than the new rating.

The official handicapper and the punter alike face difficult tasks. About a quarter of all nursery runners have had only the obligatory three outings, so, the handicapper has relatively little collateral form on which to base his calculations. He has to rate the juveniles on what they have achieved to date, possibly over an inadequate trip or on going that didn't suit them. In addition, those with early season form may have already passed their physical peak whilst horses with more physical scope might, by late summer, be on the top of their form.

Sellers

As we saw in Chapter 1 sellers demand that the winner of the race is offered for auction once the race is over. The only horses that are penalised by having to carry extra weight are those that have won previously.

Claimers

Claimers are very similar, and are ideal for two year olds of medium to moderate ability that would struggle to win a novice or conditions race. These races also provide an opportunity for two year olds which are in the grip of the handicapper – that is, the handicapper has the horse's measure. Claimers require the owner to set a price at which the animal can be 'claimed' (bought) regardless of its finishing position. The lower the price set for a claimer, the less weight the horse has to carry.

The implications for backing and laying juveniles.

So let's see what this all means in terms of backing and laying juveniles. The four types of races that justify detailed examination are maiden auction races, nurseries, novice events and claimers/sellers.

Maidens

In the maiden auction races where the cheapest horses carry the lowest weights, you might expect the weight differential to favour those with the lightest load. However, the stats show that the less weight they carry the poorer their record. In fact, the slightly more expensive two year olds – those carrying moderate weights, not too much and not too little - actually have the best strike rate. For example, over the past nine years, if you had backed every maiden auction winner carrying 9 stone 1lb then you would have broken even - 16 per cent of them won. However, horses carrying more weight have a poorer record, as do those carrying less. Winners of maiden auction races have shown that they have ability but they rarely go on to perform well in Group company. No maiden auction winner has succeeded, for example, in winning the Coventry at Royal Ascot in the past 15 years. Only one has won the Queen Mary and just two have won the Norfolk.

Nurseries

Many readers will be familiar with the old adage that you should always back top weights in nurseries. Well, the good news is that it's a much better strategy than backing those carrying the weights at the bottom. The advice requires a little bit of refinement to be really useful, but let's see first of all whether it's accurate.

Top weights in nurseries usually carry 9 stone 7lbs unless they also carry a penalty (in which case they carry more weight). Analysis of over 1,600 nurseries over the past nine years shows that of the horses carrying 9 stone 7lbs exactly, nearly 15 per cent won. However, you would have lost money if you had backed all of them.

Interestingly, the shorter the trip, the better these top weights do. In five furlong nurseries, for example, 20 per cent of horses carrying 9 stone 7lbs won, delivering a profit of £47 (to a £1) but in six, seven and eight furlong races the percentages diminish and losses are incurred. Table 26 shows the percentage strike rate at five, six, seven and eight furlongs for horses carrying 9 stone 7lbs.

Table 26 : Strike rates for top weight horses over distances 5 to 8 furlongs

	5 furlongs	6 furlongs	7 furlongs	8 furlongs
Horses carrying 9st 7lb % strike rate (winners to runners and profit or loss (£1)	20% +£47	15% -£49	13% -£114	12% -£87
Horses carrying 9-0 to 9-7 % winners to runners	15%	13%	12%	11%
Horses carrying 8-8 to 8-13 % winners to runners	10%	7%	7%	8%
Horses carrying 8-0 to 8-7 % winners to runners	7%	7%	6%	5%

POINTERS

Backing top weights in five furlong nurseries appears to pay dividends, but this diminishes over longer distances and as the season progresses.

Of the horses that carried *over* 9 stone 7lbs, 25 per cent of them won, but you would have only broken even if you'd backed them all blindly. Sticking with horses within 5lbs of the top weight delivers around half of all nursery winners. By contrast, less than five per cent of those with weights of 7st 11lbs or less were able to win.

It is possible to further refine this 'top weights in nurseries' theory for better gains, if you exclude fillies. For starters, fillies have a markedly poorer strike rate in nurseries than colts but they're also less able to carry top weight. Of the few fillies that have tried to carry more than 9 stone 7lbs, in recent years, none have won. They do win with 9 stone 7lbs, but their strike rate is markedly lower than for males. Of the fillies that carry this weight some 12 per cent succeeded, whereas 15 per cent of the colts were successful (over five - eight furlongs).

POINTERS

If you are going to back top weights, then stick with the males. Alternatively, it pays to lay fillies carrying more than 9 stone or rated higher than 90.

Backing un-exposed two year olds in nurseries (three previous runs) is also thought to be a good strategy. However, the evidence shows that this advice is incorrect. In fact, you would lose money punting blindly on juveniles that had had only three runs before their handicap debut.

POINTERS

Be wary of backing two year olds in nurseries with just three runs under the belt. But if they are a once or twice raced winner, then they deserve respect.

There is, however, one group of nursery runners that do have a better strike rate. These are the previous winners (for example of maidens) that went straight into nurseries, with only one or two runs under their belt. The few that have had only one previous run fare best of all, with 18 per cent of them winning, whilst previous winners, having had two earlier races, score on 15 per cent of the times they try. By contrast, those with 10 earlier races seem to be in the complete grip of the handicapper: only six per cent succeed.

Two year olds that carry a penalty in a nursery (that is, they have won a previous nursery) also seem to fare reasonably well. Just over 20 per cent of them go on to score again, albeit that they're usually a short price. Needless to say it doesn't pay to back them blindly but over a quarter of the horses that carry a 7lb penalty win so they should be respected.

Backing favourites from the bigger yards in nurseries can also pay dividends. With large strings of two year olds in their care, these trainers will soon spot when the handicapper has let one in too lightly. John Gosden and Jeremy Noseda have an impressive 46 per cent strike rate with their favourites in nurseries, whilst both Michael Bell and Brian Meehan hit the target with

40 per cent or more of theirs. Although the top yards find it relatively easy to assess the under-rating of their juveniles by the handicapper, there are also some very shrewd trainers with smaller strings that know what it takes to win in a nursery.

Amongst these 'dark horses' of the training ranks are Tom Dascombe who has won with 57 per cent of his nursery favourites and has won with 27 per cent of his runners in these handicaps, showing a £44 profit for a £1 stake.

Brian Meehan's statistics include a nursery winner for me several years ago that was 9/2 favourite, top-weight and stepping up in trip for the first time from five to six furlongs. The horse, called *See In The Dark*, won the first nursery of the season under an inspired ride by Frankie Dettori. The winning distances were a short-head, short-head, head, head and short-head. You don't get many closer finishes than that so Matthew Tester, the two year old handicapper, must have been very pleased with the outcome. My co-owners and I were also pretty pleased with the result and Frankie gave us one of his famous flying dismounts on his return to the winner's enclosure.

Claimers

Like nurseries, it pays to stick with class. As with the shorter distance nurseries, top weights do well and those carrying below 8 stone 5lbs have a poor record. The top weights in claimers win on 18 per cent of occasions but it's possible to improve on this result by just sticking with horses rated 74 or above. These better rated animals win on more than a third of the times they try, providing a level stake profit of £45 (to £1) over the past nine years.

POINTERS

Top weights win almost one in five claimers.

Whilst reviewing relatively low grade races, like claimers, it's worth touching on the use of blinkers and visors since they are often used first time up in these races. Blinkers and visors help a horse to concentrate since they restrict the view and make the animal focus ahead down the track rather than on the other horses nearby. The downside is that their application can cause the horse to run too free, burning up essential energy too quickly.

In the UK, they can be seen as a bit of a rogue's badge and, in claimers and sellers, the use of blinkers might be a last resort when all else has failed to get the horse galvanised. However, in the US, they are a common occurrence and they don't carry the same stigma as in Britain.

I used to own a fairly moderate horse called *Dangerous Liaison* which was well placed by Brian Meehan to win three races as a juvenile. Early on in his career, he won without headgear but it soon become apparent that he was losing interest. The first time blinkers were applied, it didn't seem to do the trick but Brian persevered and under strong rides by Brett Doyle, he won a claimer and a seller, in both instances carrying top-weight. But, despite this evidence that headgear does make a difference, backing two year olds wearing blinkers first time isn't very wise. The strike rate of first-time blinkers in nurseries is only seven per cent of winners to runners and in other two year old races eight per cent. In fact, the only category of race where their application delivers a level stake profit is in two year old claimers. Maybe horses need time to get used to them, like *Dangerous Liaison*.

POINTERS

Backing juveniles wearing blinkers first time out is not a winning strategy.

Summary and conclusions about weight

So why should top weights do better, especially when the nurseries first start? Well, one of the most cogent explanations I've heard is that the better the racehorse the easier it is to disguise his or her true ability from the handicapper. It may be easier for the handicapper to establish an accurate rating for the weaker horses than get it right for the more progressive, classier types.

A racehorse is declared the winner whether it scores by a nose or nine lengths. Furthermore, the better the animal, the more easily and effortlessly it covers the ground. A classy two year old will have a higher cruising speed. A lesser animal will have to struggle to match the pace. The jockey's only task is to beat the opposition and there are no extra rewards for doing the fastest lap. It therefore follows that it's a much tougher task to assess the handicap rating of an easy winner than one that was all-out to win by a short-head.

To illustrate this, some years ago, a top jockey returned from riding one of mine in a maiden to whisper "I could have finished a little closer to the winner but I was protecting your future handicap mark." I hadn't asked him to do so. In fact I was rather hoping we'd win, but it does illustrate the tough task that the handicapper faces.

POINTERS

In nurseries, the better horses are probably under-rated, whilst the lesser animals are not.

The penalty

Penalties for a win can range from a mere 2lbs up to 14lbs, but it's very rare to see two year olds carry more than 7lbs. So does this extra weight make a difference and if so, who's favoured? My analysis suggests that most winners of novice races manage to cope with a 4lb penalty (27 per cent of those carrying 4lbs win their races) but 6lbs or more is a struggle, unless the horse is ridden by an apprentice who can use his weight allowance to reduce the burden. Carriers of 2lb penalties do no better than maidens, and debutants also have a poor strike rate. Worst of all are unpenalised winners of claimers and sellers who just seem outclassed.

The handicap

Another way of looking at weight is to check out the official handicapper's ratings rather than the physical load each horse is set to carry. Nowadays, horses rated below 45 struggle to get a run. To win a two year old seller, a horse probably needs to have ability equivalent to a rating of between 50 and 60. By contrast, an average maiden winner might be rated at 70 or more; a novice or conditions race winner might later get a rating of 80 plus; listed class two year olds tend to be rated above 95 and Group winners over 100. Not many nursery runners participate with a rating higher than 95 and, later in the season, many nurseries are restricted to juveniles with a rating of 85 or lower.

In all cases, it is patently clear that the better rated animals do best. Of the juveniles rated above 95 that ran in nurseries, around 17 per cent won. The percentage is even higher for 95 rated two year olds at 22 per cent, showing a £36 profit (to £1).

Even 85 rated juveniles have a 16 per cent strike rate which is significantly higher than those below them. Amongst the top trainers, few would show a level stake of profit if you backed each of their nursery runners. The three exceptions are Paul Cole, Sir Michael Stoute and Saeed Bin Suroor (from very few nursery runners). When Hannon, Johnston, Gosden and Meehan run a two year old in a nursery, when it has had less than three runs, then the horse should be strongly respected.

CHAPTER 7

Betting

BETTING

In the earlier chapters, I set out ways to distinguish the potential winners from the no-hopers. In this chapter, I explain some of the principles of betting and show how odds are compiled. An understanding of this can add to the likelihood of a profitable return and contribute significantly to a better chance for the punter.

So far, my aim has been to show how the probability of a two year old winning is dictated by a relatively small number of variables. Information about all these can be found on the web in *The Racing Post* or *Raceform*.

Although many punters see betting on two year olds as very difficult, the accessibility of the information makes the betting challenge much easier. Once you know the statistics, it starts to look like a more manageable challenge altogether. It ceases to look like a lottery. However, there are other pretty compelling reasons why specialising in this sector of the sport can be rewarding both mentally as well as materially. By appreciating the subtleties one can make more effective value judgements and bet accordingly.

First of all, I want to explain some of the ways that the odds are compiled, and the factors that influence this. Bookmakers don't just price up horses on the basis of their own specialist horse knowledge. The odds also take account of punter mentality.

How the punter influences the odds

Most betting shop customers base their selections on relatively simple criteria. They might include selections offered by newspaper tipsters, or particular trainer/jockey combinations. The bookies know this and they try to price up accordingly. They know punters at certain meetings will back famous jockeys regardless of their chances, and are likely to be very careful in relation to setting odds. Their rapid reaction to *The Racing Post*'s 'Pricewise' selections which results in a slashing of the odds on a Saturday is one obvious example of a market correction based on anticipated betting activity.

The first stage to understand is how the betting forecasts get into the papers. Nowadays, there are only two organisations that produce betting forecasts; the Press Association (PA) and *The Racing Post*. The PA has a unique position in the sport since it is the official supplier of racecard data and Starting Price returns to all news outlets.

The PA starts the work of pricing up each race as soon as the five day declarations are available, using a mixture of computer models and human judgement. As soon as the overnight declarations are published, the odds compilers start creating a revised betting forecast so that the data can be despatched swiftly for publication in evening papers.

Jockey booking tend to be finalised slightly later in the day and, if some look significant, then the PA will revise its betting forecasts in time for dispatch to race day new outlets (national newspapers and the like). This version is available by 5pm each evening.

In tandem with this, *The Racing Post*'s odds compilers are producing their own betting forecasts based on their own expert knowledge. Again, these guides are available on line by late afternoon prior to the race day in question.

How the exchanges influence the odds

A second important influence on the bookmakers pricing strategy is the odds available on the betting exchanges and, in particular, by Betfair. How these two parts of the market interact is important since it can guide us towards winners and highlight when odds are artificially low or disproportionately high. In other words, where there is punting value.

At around 6pm, Betfair opens its markets on the following day's horseracing. This provides an opportunity for braver market makers to start testing the water by offering tentative prices. Some use 'robot' computer programmes to provide small stake betting opportunities at prohibitively poor odds. The computer geeks and betting market traders make money by ensuring that the margins are stacked significantly in their favour. Just as importantly, they play a vital role in forming the initial market and providing the framework for the ultimate odds on offer.

By breakfast the following morning, there is some basic liquidity: that is, enough opportunity to back and/

or lay horses for reasonable sums of money in the exchanges and this provides a vital guide to bookmakers. Although most of them won't admit it, the odds compilers at the big bookmaking chains will use Betfair as a strong guide to their opening prices. What they can also see on the exchanges is the amount of money that's queuing up to go on specific horses. An excellent guide to what is fancied.

POINTERS

Check on how much money is queuing up on Betfair for specific horses.

The more there is, the more it's fancied.

The Betfair graphs, reflecting price movement and volume of money, are further evidence of what's fancied and what's not. But don't assume every drifter in the betting market is not attempting to win. In some instances, the drift might just reflect poor pricing at the beginning of the day, or the fact that the connections don't punt heavily. In the old days, the bookies needed a source of information about the horses in every racing yard, but nowadays they don't need to bother since the betting exchanges act as their guide.

With the advent of the betting exchanges, it's become much easier for the authorities to monitor betting patterns and they can see when unusual market movements occur. Although bad losers will always claim that the sport is crooked when fancied horses get beaten, I sense that the process has never been fairer or more transparent. Indeed, it is a testament to the effectiveness and the power of the tools at the disposal of the BHA that we're seeing more cases being investigated rather than fewer.

How odds translate into percentage profit for the bookmaker

It's also worth understanding a little about the odds and how they translate into percentages that dictate a bookmarker's hypothetical profit margin. In the racing world, the odds are merely an expression or interpretation of a horse's chance of winning. Every runner in every race has a chance of success, however slim. By backing a particular horse, we're basically concluding that the odds on offer underestimate the likelihood of a victory. Conversely, by laying it at a price, we're saying that its chance of winning is more remote than the odds on offer for a win.

The betting market works on percentages, which ensure a certain profit margin for the bookmaker, known as an over-round. Bookmakers turn these percentages into the odds we see in the betting shops. If you convert them back into percentages then it becomes clear that the combined total is always significantly greater than 100 per cent.

The best way to illustrate this is in a hypothetical two horse race in which each animal is of equal ability. This gives each a 50/50 chance of winning. Each horse should arguably, one might think, be priced at even money. However, this would provide no profit margin for the bookie. He'd simply have to pay the money he made on the loser straight out to the punter who backed the winner. What he does instead, is offer them both at a shade of odds-on, say 10/11, ensuring that, whatever the outcome, he still keeps something for himself.

In a race with more runners if the bookies offer a horse at even money, it suggests that they believes the horse has a 50/50 chance of winning. Looked at another way, it means they expect half their liabilities to be on this horse alone. In the case of a 6/4 chance, they anticipate 40 per cent of their liabilities to be on this animal, whilst a 9/1 shot will account for 10 per cent of their financial exposure. Odds-on shots represent an even greater liability. A horse priced at 1/4 should represent 80 per cent of the cash they take in their satchel.

Table 27 sets out the relationship between the betting odds, which are usually expressed as fractions, and the bookmaker's estimated chance (per cent) of success.

Bookmakers can, of course, price up on the basis of their judgement rather than anticipated market forces and, in many cases, they do. They won't want to be overly generous on horses they fancy even if the public doesn't appear to have latched on.

Outsiders are another good example of the bookmaker making a judgement call. In the betting ring, outsiders are rarely pushed out to the prices available on the Tote or Betfair, despite the fact that many go unbacked, since bookmakers use these runners as a means of improving their margins. The beauty of the betting exchanges, if you want to lay horses, is that you're not obliged to price up every horse, unlike conventional bookies.

Table 27: The betting odds and the percentage chance of winning

ODDS ON %	PRICE	ODDS AGAINST %
50.0	Evens	50.0
52.4	11/10	47.6
54.5	6/5	45.5
55.6	5/4	44.4
57.9	11/8	42.1
60.0	6/4	40.0
61.9	13/8	38.1
63.6	7/4	36.4
65.2	15/8	34.8
66.7	2/1	33.3
69.2	9/4	30.8
71.4	5/2	28.6
73.3	11/4	26.7
75.0	3/1	25.0
76.9	10/3	23.1
77.8	7/2	22.2
80.0	4/1	20.0
81.8	9/2	18.2
83.3	5/1	16.7
84.6	11/2	15.4
85.7	6/1	14.3
86.7	13/2	13.3
87.5	7/1	12.5
88.3	15/2	11.7
88.9	8/1	11.1
89.5	17/2	10.5
90.0	9/1	10.0

90.9	10/1	9.1
91.7	11/1	8.3
92.3	12/1	7.7
93.3	14/1	6.7
94.1	16/1	5.9
94.7	18/1	5.3
95.2	20/1	4.8
95.8	22/1	4.2
96.2	25/1	3.8
96.6	28/1	3.4
97.0	33/1	3.0
97.6	40/1	2.4
98.0	50/1	2.0
98.5	66/1	1.5
98.8	80/1	1.2
99.0	100/1	1.0

Understanding market forces

Understanding the odds and how they are derived is one thing. Appreciating the market moves and their significance to two year old races is another matter altogether.

Fancied runners in two year old, non-handicap, races have an excellent record with favourites winning 40 per cent of the time. The challenge is to know when to back them and when to stay clear. The pointers set out earlier in the book enable some of the favourites to be eliminated, but the market can also give us further important clues. Using *The Racing Post*'s forecast odds, I've analysed over 530 two year old non-handicaps over three recent seasons. The results provide interesting reading.

What the results show first and foremost, is that *The Racing Post*'s odds compilers should be congratulated on doing a pretty good job. They correctly forecasted the favourites on nearly 75 per cent of occasions. But when the money on race day starts talking for a different horse, a different favourite emerges. On these occasions about a third of them go on to win – but of course, two thirds do not. They are beaten, some of them by the favourite that was forecast in the morning paper.

POINTERS

When the market creates a different favourite than that listed in *The Racing Post* then it deserves considerable respect.

Drifting and deposed favourites (based on *The Racing Post*'s odds forecast) do win their share of races but only about 20 per cent are successful. This success rate diminishes the more the horse's price drifts. But when the newspaper's forecast favourite holds its price or shortens then this market confidence is reflected in the results, with around 40 per cent going on to victory.

On the occasions when the favourite gets beaten, it's interesting to note that around 60 per cent of the winners had a significantly shorter starting price than that shown in *The Racing Post*'s odds forecast.

POINTERS

If you don't fancy the favourite then look for the other horses that are being backed.

Summing up: what is the best strategy to use?

Understanding the betting market is a complex business and I don't pretend to appreciate all its subtleties. However, it is clear in two year old non-handicaps that watching the market moves can help you to find a winner.

Market opposition can be due to a lack of stable confidence but it can also reflect interest in another runner, with bookmakers pushing out the price of other horses in an attempt to attract money. When *Wave Aside* won for us at Newbury in 2008, he drifted from 8/1 to 9/1 despite considerable stable confidence.

A process of elimination

I prefer to approach winner finding via a process of elimination. Firstly, by taking out the horses that appear to have little chance of success, one is left with a much smaller field on which to focus attention. Such a strategy also provides a potential list of horses that can be laid on the exchanges. In the following paragraphs, I provide a checklist of the pointers, which, together with a review of the betting market, can further highlight the horses that seem favoured by conditions or fancied by connections.

Racecourse
Factors to consider: state of the ground; influence of the draw; specific characteristics of the track; suitability for debutants (especially if drawn wide); long distance travellers; class of race and performance of favourites.

Paddock inspection
Factors to consider: good muscle tone (condition); shiny coat; bright eyes; alert but relaxed manner; not too leggy, lean or weak; and not agitated, sweating or whinnying.

Breeding
Factors to consider: birthdate; stallion suitability (precocious progeny, stamina index, win rate first time out and going preferences); the dam's credentials, and temperament.

Trainers
Factors to consider: expertise with two year olds; first time strike rate (by racecourse); betting market expectations; second time strike rate (by racecourse); finishing position of the horse first time out; the yard's recent success rate; monthly success rates, and the seven day rule.

Jockeys

Factors to consider: racecourse success on juveniles, and seven pound claimers.

Weight

Factors to consider: race conditions and weight implications; top weights; colts versus fillies; exposed versus unexposed; penalties; performance of the top yards, and headgear.

CHAPTER 8

Top Race Profiles

TOP RACE PROFILES

Some races seem more often than others to be won by horses with distinct profiles. In others races, a winning profile is less clear. In this chapter, my aim is to identify the distinct characteristics, where the evidence suggests there are trends. I have set out evidence relating to the top 37 two year old races to help the punter understand what to back and what to lay.

Every horse entered in the top two year old races is there to win, even if its chance looks remote on paper. Nevertheless, it is true that the winners of the top races often display similar characteristics, making it possible to shortlist those entries whose credentials match. Equally relevant, for those using the betting exchanges are the horses whose profiles fail to fit. Occasionally, there is no fit amongst any of the runners and, inevitably, the surprise outcome is difficult to predict.

In each of the following 37 races I have examined the trends over the 15 most recent occasions that the races have been run (excluding occasions when the race has been moved due to water logging or building works, such as at Ascot in 2005). In each case, I describe the general characteristics of the race, followed by the indicators of a good performance and the indicators associated with a poor performance.

Hilary Needler Trophy: Beverley

The first really significant two year old race of the season is the Hilary Needler Trophy over a stiff five furlongs at Beverley. This listed contest takes place in late May or early June and attracts useful fillies who can go on to win at Royal Ascot before competing in other important two year old races. Over the years, there have been a few upsets, most notably, when horses drawn low (near the stands rail) have succeeded in overcoming this negative draw to win. However, on each occasion when there was such an upset, there were 12 or more runners. When there are fewer runners, the high drawn horses tend to dominate.

POSITIVE INDICATORS	NEGATIVE INDICATORS
Lightly raced (two or fewer outings).	Two year olds who have already had a lot of racing.
Debutants can win but recent changes to winners' penalties should favour those with some experience.	A stamina index under 6.5 furlongs.
Stamina to climb the stiff 5 furlongs (most are by sires with a stamina index of 7.0 or higher).	A penalty for an earlier win is an impediment (but the penalty requirements may be changing in 2009).
Northern trainers (e.g. Tim Easterby).	An outside draw unless there are 12 or more runners.
A birthday in March or earlier.	
. Almost all winners had had a 10 day break or more since their last run.	No May foal has won in recent years and April foals have a disappointing record.
Those drawn nearest to the far rail.	It is very rare to have run or won over 6 furlongs previously.
If they've run then they need to have won.	It's very difficult to make all.

National Stakes: Sandown

The National Stakes is another important two year old race for early season sprinters. It also takes place in late May or early June and is open to both colts and fillies. This race is a good pointer to Royal Ascot since the stamina required to win over Sandown's stiff five furlongs is ideal for Ascot's straight. However, the nature of the Sandown sprint track makes it very difficult for a two year old to lead from start to finish. No winner of the National Stakes has succeeded in making all the running during the last 15 years so avoid juveniles that like to lead from the front. The draw is also very significant on good or softer ground, favouring those with a high number.

POSITIVE INDICATORS	NEGATIVE INDICATORS
Lightly raced (3 or fewer outings).	Horses that have had 4 outings or more.
Fillies and penalised animals (but the penalty requirements may be changing in 2009).	A stamina index under 6.5.
Nearly all winners have been by stallions with a stamina index of 7.0 or higher.	Horses drawn one in fields of eight or more.
Southern trainers (e.g. Richard Hannon).	Horses that have been competing in low class races (class 5 and 6).
A birthday in March or earlier.	Juveniles who have made all in earlier races.
Colts can win within seven days of a previous run but most have had 12 days or more off.	
A place in the first four last time out.	
Maidens can win.	

Woodcote Stakes: Epsom

The Woodcote Stakes at Epsom on Derby Day in June is the first listed contest over six furlongs for two year olds. Despite the sharp nature of the track, this race is quite a stamina test and not all runners see out the distance. The steep downhill bend into the straight and the pronounced camber can also cause problems, especially on fast ground. Two year olds also need to cope with the huge crowds, the noise and the colour. This is not an easy race to win.

POSITIVE INDICATORS	NEGATIVE INDICATORS
Always lightly raced (3 or fewer outings).	Maidens who've had more than one run.
A previous winner that was first or second on its last outing.	Fillies can win but they have a poor strike rate.
Maidens that have had only one previous run.	Horses can make all but it's not common to win from the front.
Unpenalised animals have won half the recent races (but the penalty requirements may be changing in 2009).	Those with a stamina index of less than 7.0.
Those carrying 5lbs extra as opposed to those carrying an additional 3lbs.	Nearly all winners had had at least a 10 day break since their last race so avoid quick returners.
A previous run over six furlongs (half the winners).	Horses that have won a class 6 contest.
A stamina index of 7.0 or more.	
A draw in the lowest three stalls.	

Coventry Stakes: Royal Ascot

It takes a seriously good two year old to win the Coventry Stakes at Royal Ascot and many go on to perform with credit in Group 1 contests. The stiff uphill climb makes this six furlong race a real test of stamina and it suits horses that are mature both physically and mentally. More often than not, the winners have already had a couple of outings and are race hardened. The race is much tougher for horses that have only had one previous outing since they need to have learnt how to battle. Facile winners of an earlier race, who beat moderate opposition, can lack the necessary fighting skills to be really competitive.

POSITIVE INDICATORS	NEGATIVE INDICATORS
Lightly raced and nearly always just one or two earlier outings.	Maidens and fillies.
An impressive win last time out.	All May born runners.
A previous win over 6 furlongs (one previous winner had won over 7f) at class 4 or better.	Horses that have already had four outings.
A stamina index of 8.0 or more.	Horses that make all.
A birthday before the end of March.	Woodcote runners.
A draw close to either running rail.	
Their last race in May or early June and/or a 20 day break since their last run.	
Aidan O'Brien has an outstanding record.	
Horses that can come from behind.	

Windsor Castle Stakes: Royal Ascot

The Windsor Castle Stakes became a listed race in 2004, which has changed its complexion, but some useful pointers are still relevant. The Windsor Castle tends to be the poor relation of the Norfolk Stakes, attracting the out and out sprint two year olds that aren't quite good enough to compete in Group company. However, smart animals can still win, provided they are not heavily penalised for earlier success.

POSITIVE INDICATORS	NEGATIVE INDICATORS
Lightly raced but having had a couple of outings.	Horses that have had four or more previous outings.
Maidens that have been second in an earlier race.	A 4lb penalty (but the penalty requirements may be changing in 2009).
A racing career that began in mid-April with an outing in late May or early June, plus a two week break or more since the last run.	Fillies used to have a good record but haven't done well recently.
A birthday in March or earlier.	Debutants can win but it hasn't happened in recent years.
A stamina index of 7.0 or higher.	May foals.
It is possible to make all.	

Queen Mary Stakes: Royal Ascot

The Queen Mary tends to attract the best of the five furlong fillies and is always an excellent contest. Fields of 15 or more are the norm and the first and second are often drawn adjacent to each other. Certain earlier races in the season have proved to be important stepping stones to victory. The Hilary Needler and National Stakes are excellent examples, provided there's been a three week break before the Royal Ascot meeting. A conditions race at Newbury in May has also delivered the Queen Mary winner on several occasions.

POSITIVE INDICATORS	NEGATIVE INDICATORS
Proven ability in conditions races or listed contests.	Maidens. May foals.
Having had just one or two runs and an unbeaten record.	6 furlong winners have a poor record but can win.
A stamina index of 7.0 or more. A birthday in March or earlier.	Horses that like to make all, though this is easier to do on fast ground.
A first race in May, usually at a top track, and a two week break prior to Ascot.	Winners of class 5 or 6 races have a very poor record.
A previous win over a stiff five furlongs, or if beaten, then it needs to have been in listed company.	It is rare to have had more than three earlier outings (*Gilded* in 2006 being a very notable exception.)

Norfolk Stakes: Royal Ascot

Winners of the Norfolk used to be race hardened sprinters with several runs already under their belt but, in recent years, typical victors have been much more lightly raced. Either way, it's always a previous winner, mostly at a stiff five furlong track or over an easy six furlongs that takes top place.

POSITIVE INDICATORS	NEGATIVE INDICATORS
Winners can have had up to four runs previously but if they've had 3 or more they've almost invariably won two of them.	Maidens have a very poor record.
	Soft ground for an out and out sprinter.
A stamina index as low as 6.5.	
	The draw used to favour those drawn low but now it seem irrelevant.
Winners of a conditions race or listed contest.	
Fillies can win but rarely take part.	Horses that ran in a Royal Ascot race earlier in the week.
A multiple race winner.	
	Horses that have done all their winning at sharp tracks.
Favourite status in their previous race.	
Winners can have raced within the past 12 days.	

Chesham Stakes: Royal Ascot

The Chesham has the curious condition of being open only to two year olds sired by horses that previously won over a mile and a quarter or further. The race also changed its distance from six to seven furlongs in 1996 so the winners now require considerable stamina. This tends to result in very lightly raced horses competing, but a few trends have emerged over the years.

POSITIVE INDICATORS	NEGATIVE INDICATORS
Fewer than two previous outings.	Debutants – have won but it's very difficult for them.
A win if two previous races have been run.	Maidens – if they have had no more than one outing.
Maidens and fillies.	Horses that have run in the Woodcote.
A previous win over six or possibly seven furlongs.	
A birthday in March or earlier although a May born juvenile did win in 2008.	
A stamina index in excess of 9.0.	
A high draw.	
Winners tend to come from the first three in the betting.	
Winners can have run 10 days earlier but most had a break of 20 days or more.	

Albany Stakes: Royal Ascot

This fillies only six furlong race is relatively new to the Ascot agenda, having first taken place in 2002, but it always attracts a high class field and was promoted to Group 3 in 2005. Trends are still emerging but there are a few pointers that can help.

POSITIVE INDICATORS	NEGATIVE INDICATORS
Lightly raced with just one or two earlier outings. A history of being placed in earlier races. A stamina index of around 8.0 or higher. A birthday in March or earlier. A previous outing over six furlongs. An 18 day break since their last race.	Fillies that have had more than two runs or who are debutants. A cheap purchase price. Horses bred to be sprinters. Horses that have won over an easy 5 furlongs.

Cherry Hinton Stakes: Newmarket

This race tends to be the next step in the season for fillies that have won or run in the Queen Mary or Albany. However, unlike these Royal Ascot races, where all horses run unpenalised, the Cherry Hinton places a 3lb burden on winners of Group 1 and 2 races. This makes it tough for Queen Mary winners since they are forced to carry a penalty. Like most of the two year old races at Royal Ascot, this race tends to be won by lightly raced animals.

POSITIVE INDICATORS	NEGATIVE INDICATORS
Only one or two previous outings.	Maidens and fillies that have had more than four runs.
At least one previous win.	Fillies by stallions with a stamina index below 6.5.
A career start no earlier than May or June.	Fillies born late April and May.
A stamina index of 7.0 or more.	
A birthday in March or earlier.	The draw seems to vary and can be influenced by the position of the running rail, so check on the day of the race.
At least 10 days since their last run.	
Form over six furlongs.	It is possible to carry a 3lb penalty but few try and most fail.

July Stakes: Newmarket

Somewhat surprisingly, the six furlong July Stakes gets as many winners from the five furlong Norfolk Stakes as from the six furlong Coventry Stakes. But not all the winners of this race have shown ability at the Royal meeting. If they haven't run in the Norfolk then they will almost certainly have run over six furlongs at another racecourse.

POSITIVE INDICATORS	NEGATIVE INDICATORS
Lightly raced (one or two previous outings).	Horses that have had four or more outings.
Maidens that have been second in a race previously.	Horses that have had just one run.
A stamina index of over 7 or better still over 8.	Coventry Stakes winners haven't won this race since 1989 but not many try.
Winners can carry a 3lb penalty.	
A birthday in March or earlier (but May born juveniles have won).	
A win or a place over six furlongs.	
A break of around 20 days or more since the last run.	

Superlative Stakes: Newmarket

The Superlative Stakes shifted from being a listed race in 2002, to a Group 3 in 2003 and then it became a Group 2 from 2006. These rapid upgrades are clear evidence that the racing authorities believe the race is attracting increasingly classy animals. However, there have also been changes to the race conditions that make it difficult to compare winners over the years. Past winners include a subsequent Derby winner and an Irish 2000 Guineas winner, so it's clear that it now takes a smart animal to win it.

POSITIVE INDICATORS	NEGATIVE INDICATORS
Lightly raced horses (but it is possible to win with up to 5 previous runs). A previous run over six or seven furlongs. A stamina index of 7.9 or more. At least a 10 day break and preferably a break of three weeks or more. A birthday in April, suggesting that the later maturing two year olds are starting to make their mark.	Maidens used to win but this is less likely now. Fillies have occasionally run but none has won since 1994. It used to be difficult to win carrying a penalty but Group 2 status should make this less relevant. A sire with a stamina index below 7.9.

Weatherbys Super Sprint: Newbury

Over the past few years, it's taken Royal Ascot form to win the Super Sprint but horses don't necessarily have to have been placed at the Royal meeting in order to carry off this prize. My own winner, *Siena Gold*, had disappointed in the Queen Mary Stakes, because of the very fast ground, but bounced back on the slightly easier surface at Newbury. The other important factor that helped the horse was her relatively low sales price which dictated how much weight she had to carry. Carrying top weight in this contest is no easy task and only one two year old since 1991 has managed to carry more than 8 stone 11lb to victory.

POSITIVE INDICATORS	NEGATIVE INDICATORS
Horses with three or fewer outings – although up to five is possible. Fillies do better than colts. Horses carrying 8 stone 11lbs or less, particularly if carrying 8 stone 6lbs or less. A birthday in March or earlier (but horses with April birthdays can win). A break of at least two weeks (although one winner ran only 9 days earlier). A career starting in a Class 5 race or better. A very high or a very low draw (if the ground has been watered). A previous win over a stiff five furlongs or an easy six. A first outing in late April or May. A stamina index of 7.0 or above.	Very lightly raced juveniles. Horses carrying less than 8 stone 1lb (i.e. very cheap animals). A May birthday. Maidens (except in 2005 when a 100/1 shot won). A previous win over a stiff 6 furlongs.

Princess Margaret Stakes: Ascot

The Princess Margaret Stakes on King George and Queen Elizabeth Day at Ascot, is another race that attracts its fair share of Royal Ascot runners but they tend to have a poor strike rate. Historically, winners of the Queen Mary and Albany Stakes tend to go on to race elsewhere since they have to carry a penalty in the Princess Margaret Stakes. But placed horses from the Albany Stakes have won the Princess Margaret a couple of times in recent years, so they are worthy of consideration. The same applies to winners of a six furlong fillies only maiden at Newmarket's July meeting; they have gone on to win this race on four occasions.

POSITIVE INDICATORS	NEGATIVE INDICATORS
Lightly raced (just one or two outings).	Horses with more than three previous runs.
Maidens but only if they have been placed second previously.	A penalty.
A win or a place in their previous race.	Horses that started their careers in April or early May.
A stamina index of 7.8 or above.	Five furlong specialists and horses that have made all previously.
Favourites and fancied runners (nothing larger than 12/1).	
A first run in late May, June or July.	
A previous run over six furlongs.	
A birthday in March or earlier.	

Molecomb Stakes: Goodwood

Historically, the Molecomb seemed to suit race hardened sprinters. However, in the last three years, the winners have been relatively lightly raced so the profile may be changing. Fillies have a good strike rate, having won nine out of the last fifteen runnings. However, over 40 per cent of the runners were female so this is not quite as significant a result as it first sounds. One might also expect the Molecomb to be a happy hunting ground for five furlong sprinters that have contested Royal Ascot's juvenile races or the Super Sprint. However, over the past 15 years, not one Royal Ascot or Super Sprint winner has gone on to victory in the Molecomb. Of nearly 80 Ascot runners who entered, only five succeeded. And although Super Sprint runners have a slightly better strike rate, over 85 per cent have been turned over. Perhaps these tough mid-season two year old races leave their mark or maybe the Goodwood hill finds them out. Whatever the explanation, it seems safer to lay them.

POSITIVE INDICATORS	NEGATIVE INDICATORS
Multiple winners and battle hardened sprinters but the occasional lightly-raced speedster can also win.	No maiden has won in the past 15 years.
Horses placed in the first three last time out.	The draw seems relatively insignificant but stall one wins less often than the others.
Horses that are held up.	A previous win over 6 furlongs.
Horses with two wins if they have had more than three outings.	Horses that like to make all.
A first outing from May onwards.	
Fillies do well and horses can carry a penalty.	
Sires with a stamina index below 8.0.	
A previous win over 5 furlongs.	
A March or earlier birthday.	
At least 10 days since the last run.	

Vintage Stakes: Goodwood

The Vintage Stakes has witnessed some smart winners over the years, and a number of them have gone on to classic success as three year olds. However, it's not always easy to spot them in advance. In recent years, the vast majority of Vintage Stakes victors have won little more than a maiden or conditions race previously and have yet to compete in Group company. Which is not to say that the occasional winner doesn't come via Royal Ascot or Newmarket's top two year old races but this is much rarer. Royal Ascot runners – as opposed to Royal Ascot winners – have a particularly bad strike rate. Over the past 15 years, 26 horses have come on from the Royal meeting to race in the Vintage Stakes and only two have been successful.

POSITIVE INDICATORS	NEGATIVE INDICATORS
Lightly raced (no more than three outings).	Maidens. The only one that has won was placed second in its only other race.
Prior success over 6 or 7 furlongs.	Fillies very rarely run and haven't won in the past 15 years.
Those with three earlier races tend to have won two.	
A win last time out.	Carrying a penalty (only two out of eleven succeeded).
A stamina index of 7.0 or over.	A previous win at 5 furlongs (only one success).
A high draw.	
A birthday in March or earlier, although April or May born juveniles can win.	
At least a 10 day break since their last run.	
Horses that are held up.	

Richmond Stakes: Goodwood

Royal Ascot is a popular stepping-stone for the Richmond Stakes but Ascot runners don't have the best of strike rates, even though in 2007 and 2008 horses placed at the Royal meeting went on to win it. In the past fifteen years only four juveniles out of 40 Royal Ascot runners have won the Richmond. The more typical profile for the race is a lightly raced colt that's stepping up from a novice or conditions race. The other factor to bear in mind for the Richmond is that Goodwood has a distinct downhill gradient. Not all horses cope. This means that past course winners should be respected, as should other runners which are already proven downhill. For example, Newmarket winners, where there is a distinct dip, seem to handle the Goodwood gradient well.

POSITIVE INDICATORS	NEGATIVE INDICATORS
Horses that have won previously at Goodwood or Newmarket.	Maidens (not since 1989).
Lightly raced (a maximum of 4 previous runs).	Royal Ascot runners.
A win or a place last time out.	A penalty.
A stamina index of between 6.4 and 8.7.	Horses that have been on the go since early April.
A late start to the racing career (no runs until mid-May).	A draw in stall one.
A previous run over 6 furlongs.	A birthday in May.
At least a 10 day break.	A horse that makes all.
A high draw.	A horse with Group form.
A birthday in March or earlier (although April foals can win).	

Sweet Solera Stakes: Newmarket

Like the seven furlong Vintage Stakes at Goodwood, the Sweet Solera Stakes attracts horses with stouter pedigrees and 'classic' aspirations but, in this instance, the race is restricted to fillies only. The race has been won in the past by several horses that have gone on to win Group 1 contests, and it was therefore (justifiably) upgraded to Group 3 in 2004. Winners tend to be lightly raced, progressive types that have yet to show their true ability. Most victors are previous maiden winners but several successful horses have come out of a Sandown seven furlong listed contest that takes place in July.

POSITIVE INDICATORS	NEGATIVE INDICATORS
Lightly raced (1 or 2 outings). Fillies with just one previous run are almost always previous winners. A stamina index of at least 8, or 9 or more. Proven over 6 or 7 furlongs. A career that started in a class 4 race or better. A birthday before the end of March.	Maidens (but can't be ruled out entirely). Fillies with more than three previous outings. A penalty. A draw in stall one. A birthday in May.

Acomb Stakes: York

The Acomb Stakes has only recently been given Group 3 status but deservedly so since it's been won by some very smart performers in recent years, some of which have gone on to win at the very highest level. Most recent winners have been lightly raced types moving up from maiden company but this profile might start to shift now that listed winners are unpenalised.

POSITIVE INDICATORS	NEGATIVE INDICATORS
No more than two previous outings.	Fillies.
A previous win or placed in the first three.	A history of having started in class 6 or lower.
A stamina index over 8.0.	Anything less than a 10 day break since the last run.
A previous run over 7 furlongs, although a few were stepping up from 6.	A stamina index less than 7.6.
Fancied runners.	
A high draw.	
Born in March or earlier although horses born in April and May can win.	

Gimcrack Stakes: York

One of the more novel aspects of the Gimcrack Stakes is that winning owners are invited to give a speech at an annual dinner held at the racecourse in December. I don't think this requirement has ever adversely influenced owners' plans to enter the race but several winning owners have passed the speaking invitation on to a nominee. Over the years the Gimcrack has become a summer racing highlight, attracting some of the best six furlong two year old colts. It has been won by some very smart animals indeed, but is only rarely won by a horse that later wins a classic. The majority of winners pursue sprint careers as three year olds.

The race tends to be made up of a mixture of group race performers and lightly raced maiden winners, with the winners coming from both camps in equal proportion. This makes it difficult to find an ideal profile but there is one statistic which is pretty compelling. Horses that have run at 'Glorious Goodwood' earlier in the month have a dire record. You would have to go back to 1988 to find a Gimcrack winner that performed well at Goodwood's main summer meeting.

POSITIVE INDICATORS	NEGATIVE INDICATORS
Lightly raced (generally no more than three outings). A stamina index between 7 and 10. A previous run (and ideally a win) over 6 furlongs. A high draw. A win at Newmarket. A birthday in March or earlier. A minimum 10 day break since the last run.	Maidens can win it but they need to have been placed in the first three in an earlier race. Winners over 7 furlongs previously. A penalty. A birthday in May (only one win in the past 15 years).

Lowther Stakes: York

The typical profile of a Lowther Stakes winner is of a filly that has already proved herself in the very best company. Almost every year, the winner has already won or been placed in either a Royal Ascot juvenile race or the Princess Margaret Stakes. There are, of course, exceptions, and it is still not easy to weight up the relative merits of a Queen Mary winner taking on a Cherry Hinton or Princess Margaret winner but it pays to stick with the proven performers.

In the past 15 years, seven Queen Mary winners have gone on to run in the Lowther and three have succeeded. By comparison, nine Princess Margaret winners have attempted the same double and three have been successful. But both have done better than winners of the Cherry Hinton at Newmarket where only a couple of placed horses have gone on to win the Lowther. The top races with the worst record subsequently in the Lowther are the Molecomb, the Windsor Castle Stakes and the Super Sprint.

POSITIVE INDICATORS	NEGATIVE INDICATORS
Winning form.	Fillies with a sprint stallion pedigree (a stamina index below 7).
Lightly raced (3 or fewer previous outings).	
A win or a second place last time out.	May born juveniles (only one has won in the past 15 years).
A stamina index over 7.5 or better still over 8.	Horses that make all.
A penalty is not an obstacle.	
A high draw.	
A birthday in March or earlier.	
A month off since their last run.	

St. Leger Yearling Stakes: York

The St. Leger Yearling Stakes is one of the most valuable two year old races of the season, carrying a guaranteed first prize of over £150,000. Even the 10th horse in the race is guaranteed £7,500, so it's always hotly contested. For these reasons, it attracts a large entry and many would-be runners are balloted out (although there is a consolation race for most of them). Those that remain in the race are the ones that the official handicapper believes to be the best of the bunch, ensuring that the race is highly competitive.

From a trends perspective, it's a difficult race to take a view on, particularly because it's only been established for eleven years, and partly because the location of the race moved (from Doncaster to York) and its date changed. Nevertheless, there are some patterns that appear to be identifiable.

POSITIVE INDICATORS	NEGATIVE INDICATORS
A rating of 90 or more.	A penalty.
Up to four previous outings.	Fillies have a poor record, but few have run in the past few years.
A Class 4 or better win.	
A stamina index above 7.5.	A horse that makes all.
A previous race over 6 or 7 furlongs and, ideally a win over this distance.	
A birthday in April or earlier.	
A month off since the last run.	

Prestige Stakes: Goodwood

The Prestige Stakes tends to be won by progressive fillies that have yet to prove themselves in Group company. For example, in the past 15 years, three winners of the Prestige had already tried their hand in Group races but none had been successful. The majority of recent victors were just maiden winners or had been successful in conditions events. The record also sug-

gests that trainers prefer to run their best seven furlong fillies in other Group races during late summer
and only rarely does the Prestige deliver a classic winner.

POSITIVE INDICATORS	NEGATIVE INDICATORS
Only three previous outings.	Fillies carrying a penalty.
At least one win in a class 5 or better, or a place in the first three.	Horses dropping back from 8 to 7 furlongs.
A stamina index of 8.5 or higher.	A low draw in fields of nine or more runners.
A win over 6 or 7 furlongs.	
A birthday before the end of March or earlier.	
At least a two week break since the last run.	

May Hill Stakes: Doncaster

The May Hill in mid-September is one of the season's
most significant one mile races for fillies. Over the
years, this Group 2 contest has produced a number
of future classic winners and it takes some winning.
One might expect the winners to have already proved
themselves in Group company but, in the past anyway,
the May Hill has usually been won by progressive types
who have been lightly raced maiden or conditions race

winners. This is not to say that the occasional Group winner hasn't been successful, but such horses have to carry a penalty and this has tended to anchor them.

Now that the May Hill has become a Group 2 contest, winners of Group races such as the Sweet Solera Stakes at Newmarket are appearing to do better. Conversely, winners and placed fillies from Goodwood's Group 3 Prestige Stakes have an appalling record with only one success in the past 15 years. Interestingly, fillies that have won a 7 furlong maiden at Newmarket in the summer have an excellent profile for the May Hill. Seven winning fillies have done so in the last 15 years.

POSITIVE INDICATORS	NEGATIVE INDICATORS
Three or fewer outings plus multiple wins if they've had two or more runs.	Maidens.
	A penalty (although this trend may be shifting now that the race is a Group 2).
Once raced winners.	
A stamina index over 9.0.	Less than a two week break since the last race.
Favourites and fancied animals.	
	Winners and placed horses in the Prestige Stakes.
A price no higher than 9/1.	
A win or a run over 7 furlongs.	A stamina index below 7.6.
A career that didn't start until June or later.	A previous race over 8 furlongs.

Flying Childers Stakes: Doncaster

This race is sometimes billed as the 5 furlong sprint championship for two year olds but it only rarely produces a top sprinter of the future. It is, therefore, somewhat surprising that it still holds Group 2 status but there is no doubting that it takes a bit of winning. During the past 15 years, the margin of victory has only once exceeded two lengths.

The typical winner's profile is of a hardened sprinter with quite a few races under the belt that might have tried six furlongs but whose ideal trip is a flat-out five. Most years, the race is peppered with runners who've contested the better five and six furlong races such as the Royal Ascot sprints, the July Stakes, Cherry Hinton, Molecomb, Gimcrack and Lowther. The tough task is trying to work out which form is the most significant.

Sadly, there are no hard and fast rules but, when runners have won or come second in a Group race over five furlongs, then they deserve considerable respect. The Molecomb and Norfolk Stakes have the best record. Respect should also be given to any winners of the Richmond Stakes or of the listed Roses Stakes at York. Likewise, runners who were beaten in the six furlong Gimcrack or Lowther Stakes at York seem to do well for the drop back in distance. If performers in none of these are competing then expect an upset. But winners of the Newbury Super Sprint or the St. Hugh's Stakes (a listed contest over five furlongs) don't do well.

POSITIVE INDICATORS	NEGATIVE INDICATORS
At least three outings and at least one win (horses with up to nine previous outings have won).	Maidens.
	A low draw in a big fieild (over 8 runners).
Fillies in preference to colts.	Horses that make all.
A stamina index of 7.0 or more (even though this is a sprint).	A break of less than eleven days.
A penalty is not an obstacle.	
A rating of 100 or more.	
A previous win over 5 furlongs.	

Champagne Stakes: Doncaster

Most years, the seven furlong Champagne Stakes attracts performers that go on to prove themselves in Group I races and the race has seen its fair share of future classic winners. Victors tend to fall into two categories: firstly, there are lightly raced types who are progressing fast. Secondly, there are proven Group performers. On the whole, the betting market seems to know when the relatively unexposed types are good enough to win and favourites have a good record. However, winners of Group races can find it tough to carry a penalty and only around 30 per cent succeed in giving the weight. Of the five that succeeded, three had won six furlong Group races whilst the others had won at seven furlongs.

POSITIVE INDICATORS	NEGATIVE INDICATORS
Up to five previous outings is not an impediment.	Maidens.
	Horses that have won over 5 furlongs.
Horses with three or more outings who won at least two.	Doubtful stayers.
A place or a win last time out.	A stamina index below 7.8.
A stamina index over 9.	A birthday in April or May.
A previous win over 7 furlongs (some had won over 6).	
A birthday in March or earlier.	
It is possible to make all.	

Mill Reef Stakes: Newbury

Named after one of the greatest racehorses of the 20th century, the Mill Reef Stakes should be delivering classic winners on a regular basis, but you have to go back nearly 40 years to find one. Nowadays, the race tends to be won by battle-hardened two year olds that have relatively little improvement in them when they become three. There are, of course, exceptions like *Excellent Art* that went on to win the Group 1 St. James's Palace Stakes the following year. But most winners of this race are precocious two year olds that are already multiple winners over sprint distances and have the miles on the clock to prove it.

POSITIVE INDICATORS	NEGATIVE INDICATORS
Up to five previous outings.	Lightly raced and in-experienced two year olds.
Consistently winning or placed horses.	Fillies (only one in 12 has succeeded).
Colts or geldings without a penalty.	Horses carrying a penalty.
A stamina index of between 7.1 and 8.8.	A birthday in May.
Runners with an official rating above 100.	
Proven record over 6 furlongs.	
Experience in Group 1 or 2 company.	
A birthday in April or earlier.	

Royal Lodge Stakes: Ascot

The Royal Lodge Stakes is run over Ascot's Old Mile and is a severe test of stamina, especially on soft or heavy going. The race, which starts in Swinley Bottom, is uphill for most of the way, including around the home turn into the relatively short finishing straight. This is therefore also a tough race in which to carry a penalty. Over the past 15 years, seven horses have tried and none have succeeded. The ideal profile is a colt that is a listed winner or Group placed over seven furlongs or a mile. He also needs abundant stamina and relatively few miles on the clock.

POSITIVE INDICATORS	NEGATIVE INDICATORS
Four or fewer previous outings with at least one and ideally more wins.	Maidens.
	A low draw if there are more than eight runners.
A stamina index between 9 and 11.8.	
	A penalty.
A win over at least 7 furlongs.	A sire with a stamina index below 7.1.
A start to their racing career not before the end of May.	
	A birthday in May.
A birthday in March or earlier.	A horse that makes all.

Fillies Mile: Ascot

This Group I one mile race for two year old fillies has been won by many outstanding horses over the years and even placed animals have gone on to achieve classic glory. The nice thing about the Fillies Mile is that there are no penalties for previous Group success so it tends to attract some of the very best two year olds. In fact, winners tend to have proved themselves already in Group company, mostly over seven furlongs or a mile, and May Hill winners have an outstanding strike rate. Although almost all winners have been lightly raced, you have to go back to 1995 to find a winner that had only raced once before. In this particularly tough challenge, race hardened fillies seem to have an edge.

POSITIVE INDICATORS	NEGATIVE INDICATORS
No more than three runs.	Maidens.
Fillies who have had more than three runs need to have won two of them.	Fillies that just won their only outing.
A stamina index between 7.7 and 11.3.	A low draw when there are more than nine runners.
No first runs before early June – a later start is better.	Only one filly has made all in the last 15 years.
A win over 7 or 8 furlongs (or at least 6).	
May Hill winners.	
A birthday in March or earlier.	
At least 16 days since their last run.	

Cheveley Park Stakes: Newmarket

The six furlong Cheveley Park has proved itself over the years to be one of the best guides to the following season's 1000 Guineas. It tends to bring together some of the most highly tried and tested two year old fillies, as well as a few lesser animals hopeful of acquiring Group 1 'black type'. The race tends to be run at the beginning of October, which is quite late in the year for some fillies, either because they have had a long season or because they've started to grow their winter coat and this means that the race doesn't always run to form. In most seasons, however, it takes proven Group form to win. The challenge is to decipher the various form lines from Ascot, Newmarket, Doncaster, York and Goodwood.

Analysis of the outcome over the past 15 years shows that fillies who won the Queen Mary, Cherry Hinton or Princess Margaret have the best strike rate. All of these races are over stiff tracks, as is the Cheveley Park. Lowther Stakes winners (an easy six furlongs at York) can win but a lot more get beaten. Winners of the Super Sprint, Molecomb and Flying Childers seem to struggle. The Group 3 Clyde Stakes at Ayr and the listed Dick Poole Stakes at Salisbury have also produced winners but not very often. The same can be said of runners who have previously competed in the seven furlong Moyglare Stud Stakes at the Curragh or, for that matter, any seven furlong race. The drop back to six doesn't suit in most cases.

POSITIVE INDICATORS	NEGATIVE INDICATORS
No more than five previous outings.	Maidens.
Multiple previous wins if they've had two or more outings.	Horses having run just one previous race.
A stamina index in excess of 7.7.	Fillies that have already raced over 7 furlongs (1992 was the last time).
A start to their racing career not earlier than the end of May .	Horses that make all (only one succeeded in the past 15 years).
A previous race (and all bar one a win) at 6 furlongs.	
A high draw in larger fields.	
A birthday before the end of March.	
At least 10 days (and as much as three weeks) break since the previous run.	
A Group race win provided this was acquired over a stiff 5 or 6 furlongs.	

Middle Park Stakes: Newmarket

Like the Cheveley Park Stakes, this six furlong Group I race attracts some highly tried individuals. However, winners of the Middle Park Stakes only rarely win a classic. Despite this, the race has turned out some excellent sprinters. Most of these are well exposed by the time they come to the Middle Park and have already won at Group level – the Prix Morny, July Stakes, Mill Reef, Richmond, Gimcrack and Coventry, for example. My analysis suggests that the Group I Prix Morny over six furlongs at Deauville in August provides the best form because four out of seven of these winners have gone on to capture the Middle Park. Winners of the Group I Phoenix Stakes at Leopardstown over six furlongs also have an excellent record. If there's no Group I form in the race then the Coventry and Mill Reef Stakes winners tend to have the edge. Gimcrack winners have also gone on to score but winners of the July Stakes, Richmond, Flying Childers, Molecomb and Windsor Castle have not done so well.

POSITIVE INDICATORS	NEGATIVE INDICATORS
At least one win, preferably two, with one of these last time out.	Maidens.
	Horses who've had just one previous race.
A previous win at 6 (and some at 5) furlongs.	
	Horses that have competed (or won) over 7 furlongs.
Five previous runs, but not more than seven.	
	Horses that make all.
A stamina index of 7 or more, but not less than 6.7.	If they ran at Royal Ascot then they need to have won since, preferably over 6 furlongs.
A birthday in March or earlier, although April and May foals cannot be ruled out.	

Two Year Old Trophy: Redcar

Most years, the Two Year Old Trophy over six furlongs, introduced thirteen years ago, is a cavalry charge of over 20 horses and so luck in running is of paramount importance. My own runner in the race last year, called *Wave Aside*, got into a fair bit of trouble and was a shade unlucky not to win. However, he was relatively inexperienced with only two previous runs, and this goes against the typical profile for the race. Most winners have had at least five earlier outings. The race has been won by some pretty useful sprinters over the years, most of them bordering on listed class or better.

POSITIVE INDICATORS	NEGATIVE INDICATORS
At least five earlier outings and at least one win or a second over 6 furlongs.	Fillies.
An official rating above 90.	Maidens, or those who won a maiden last time out.
Carrying 9 stone or less.	Top weight (9 stone 2lbs).
Either a very high or a very low draw.	A middle draw.
Stamina is not a factor – sires had an index of between 6.3 and 8.0.	A previous race over 7 furlongs.
A birthday in April or earlier.	A birthday in May.
Group or listed form.	
Two weeks since the last run.	

Cornwallis Stakes: Ascot

The Group 3 Cornwallis Stakes over five furlongs tends to be run on good or softer ground so winners require a fair amount of stamina and an ability to act on the surface. Winners tend to be race-hardened sprinters that can dominate from the front but it's not often won by a future star. For some reason, the Cornwallis Stakes doesn't often attract Group winners over five furlongs despite the fact that they have a strong record. For example, winners of the Norfolk and Flying Childers have a good strike rate although they have to carry a penalty for their Group win. More often than not, the race attracts only listed race sprinters and on those occasions, winners of the Harry Rosebery at Ayr have an excellent record as do winners of the Roses Stakes at York, both over five furlongs. Conversely, winners of the Windsor Castle and Super Sprint appear out of their depth and Molecomb winners have a poor record.

POSITIVE INDICATORS	NEGATIVE INDICATORS
Three or more previous runs (one winner had nine).	Fillies.
At least two previous wins (one over 5 furlongs). Most also had winning or placed form over 6 furlongs.	Horses that have only won over 6 furlongs.
A stamina index of 7.1 or more.	Horses that have run over 7 furlongs.
Quite a few winners dominate the race from the start and make all.	.
Horses carrying a penalty.	
A break of two weeks since the last run.	

Dewhurst Stakes: Newmarket

The Dewhurst Stakes is rightly thought to be one of the best guides to the following year's 2000 Guineas and it is, on occasions, won by a future Derby winner. Most years, it's won by horses that have already proved themselves in Group 1 or Group 2 company over seven furlongs, for example in the National Stakes (Curragh), or the Grand Criterium (Longchamp).Overall, any seven furlong Group 1 winners have a 50 per cent strike rate.

However, there are occasions, when there is no Group 1 or 2 seven furlong winner in the field and this means that there can be the odd shock result and the punter should tread carefully. Even when there are runners with Group form in the race, finding the winner can be difficult. Some Group race winners have an appalling record. On two occasions, the winners of the Group 2 Vintage Stakes (Goodwood) got the upper hand By contrast, in the past 15 years, no previous winners of the Royal Lodge (4 tried), Middle Park (4 tried), Solario (4 tried), Coventry (4 tried), Mill Reef (3 tried), Richmond (3 tried), Superlative (3 tried) or July Stakes (3 tried) won the Dewhurst. Even the seven furlong Champagne Stakes at Doncaster has a disappointing record with only one Dewhurst winner out of eight that have tried.

POSITIVE INDICATORS	NEGATIVE INDICATORS
Group 1 form.	Maidens.
No more than 6 previous outings.	Colts with just one previous run.
Multiple winners have won 12 out of the last 15 runs.	Horses that have won over a mile.
Stamina is essential. A sire with an index of 7.8 or higher.	Horses that make all.
A rating of 100 or higher.	
A previous win over 7 furlongs (many had also won over 6).	
The draw seems of little significance.	
A birthday before the end of March.	

Rockfel Stakes: Newmarket

There's no obvious profile for Rockfel winners but the race has been won by quite a few horses that went on to be classic winners, so it's worthy of analysis. In 1998, the status of the race was raised to Group 2. This changed the penalty system and nowadays only previous Group winners are penalised. Only nine runners since 1998 have tried to give weight to their rivals and only two have succeeded. One had won a Group 1 at Longchamp earlier in the month and had little trouble giving weight to the opposition. The other had won the seven furlong Group 3 Sweet Solera at Newmarket. All other penalised Group 3 winners have been beaten, and are therefore worth opposing.

POSITIVE INDICATORS	NEGATIVE INDICATORS
A previous win.	Maidens.
No more than six previous outings.	Horses with a Group 3 penalty.
A stamina index of 7.1 or higher.	Horses that have run over a mile.
A run over 6 or 7 furlongs (or both).	Fillies that have run or won over 5 furlongs.
In the first three last time out.	
Form in Group 1 or Group 2 contests.	
Winners can make all.	
A two week break since last time out.	

Racing Post Trophy: Doncaster

Like the Rockfel, there is no immediately obvious profile for winners of the Racing Post Trophy. Some have already shown Group form ability whilst others are merely maiden winners. What we do know is that most winners are late developing types who have yet to show their true potential. For this reason, it pays to avoid horses that have already won a Group race. For example, winners of the Group 2 Royal Lodge have a poor record. Four have tried and all of them have failed as have winners of the seven furlong Beresford Stakes (six have tried but only one was successful). Winners of the Solario seem equally jinxed. If there is an exception to this, then it is probably the eight furlong Group 3 Autumn Stakes at Ascot, but relatively few horses have tried to win both races.

POSITIVE INDICATORS	NEGATIVE INDICATORS
Lightly raced.	Fillies (only one filly ran in the past 15 years but she was second).
A maximum of four previous outings.	
	Experience at 6 furlongs (though this doesn't make a win completely impossible).
Maidens if they have only had one run.	
A previous win over 7 furlongs.	A first run before late June.
	Horses that make all.
Stamina is essential so the sire has to have a stamina index in excess of 8.9.	
Previous experience over a mile isn't a disadvantage.	

Horris Hill Stakes: Newbury

The Horris Hill Stakes is not in the same class as the Dewhurst or Racing Post Trophy but it's an important two year old race all the same. The race tends to be won by progressive types that have yet to prove themselves in listed or Group company. But the occasional listed winner or Group placed horse has succeeded. What is certain, is that it is tough to carry a penalty for Group success. Only three horses have tried over the past 15 years and none has got close to winning the Horris Hill. Most winners, in fact, have previously achieved little more than a maiden win or a conditions success but they also tend to be lightly raced and learning fast.

POSITIVE INDICATORS	NEGATIVE INDICATORS
Five previous runs or fewer.	Maidens.
Multiple wins, and a win at 7 furlongs in particular.	Horses who have only raced once.
A stamina index of 7.6 or higher.	A penalty.
A start to their racing career no earlier than late June.	
A high draw when there are more than eight runners.	
An ability to act on soft or heavy ground – the usual going for this race.	